Table of Contents

Introduction

The fact that you've purchased this book means two things. The first is that you're preparing for, or at least considering taking, the TASC exam, which can open new doors for your future by greatly expanding your options for careers. The second is that you've already taken an excellent first step in picking up this study guide.

We'll provide you with a detailed overview of the TASC, so that you know exactly what to expect on test day, then we'll cover all of the subjects over which you will be tested, providing multiple practice sections for you to test your knowledge and improve. Even if it's been a while since your last major examination, don't worry; we'll make sure you're more than ready!

What is the TASC?
The TASC or "Test Assessing Secondary Completion" exam, measures your skills through the high school level in Social Studies, Science, Language Arts, Reading, Writing, and Mathematics. In short, it tests everything taught in high school, so that if you did not earn a diploma, you can still prove you have the equivalent knowledge.

Breaking Down the TASC
You will have about 7 hours to complete all sections of the test of which there are a total of approximately 235 questions. These are the sections of the TASC:

Social Studies
- 47 questions, 70 minute time limit. Tests knowledge of history, geography, economics, civics, and government.

Science
- 47 questions, 80 minute time limit. Tests knowledge of life sciences, earth, space, and physical sciences.

Reading
- 50 questions, 70 minute time limit. Tests ability to read and interpret written passages.

Mathematics
- 40 questions, 90 minute time limit. Tests knowledge of operations, measurement, geometry, algebra, data analysis, statistics, and probability.

Writing
- 50 questions,60 minute time limit. Tests knowledge of sentence structure, usage, mechanics, grammar, and organization.
- 1 essay, 50 minute time limit.

Scoring
There are two "passing" scores on the TASC. One score indicates a High School Equivalency Diploma, and the other score indicates College & Career Readiness. Different colleges will interpret these scores in different ways, so it is important to check with your local college for detailed information of what is required.

How This Book Works
The subsequent chapters in this book are divided into a review of those topics covered on the exam. This is not to "teach" or "re-teach" you these concepts – there is no way to cram all of that material into one book! Instead, we are going to help you recall all of the information that you've already learned. Even more importantly, we'll show you how to apply that knowledge.

Each chapter includes an extensive review, with practice drills at the end to test your knowledge. With time, practice, and determination, you'll be completely prepared for test day.

Chapter 1: Language Arts – The Reading Section

The TASC contains two Language Arts sections: Reading, and Writing. The Reading portion of the TASC will measure your ability to understand, analyze, and evaluate written passages. Tested passages will contain material from a variety of sources and on a number of different topics; after reading those passages, you will then have 70 minutes within which to answer 50 multiple-choice questions. In this chapter, we will discuss the various types of questions typically asked, and refresh your memory on their topics until you are confident in your ability to answer them correctly.

The Main Idea

Finding and understanding the main idea of a text is an essential reading skill. When you look past the facts and information and get to the heart of what the writer is trying to say, that's the **main idea**. Imagine that you're at a friend's home for the evening:

> "Here," he says. "Let's watch this movie."

> "Sure," you reply. "What's it about?"

You'd like to know a little about what you'll be watching, but your question may not get you a satisfactory answer, because you've only asked about the subject of the film. The subject—what the movie is about—is only half the story. Think, for example, about all the alien invasion films ever been made. While these films may share the same general subject, what they have to say about the aliens or about humanity's theoretical response to invasion may be very different. Each film has different ideas it wants to convey about a subject, just as writers write because they have something they want to say about a particular subject. When you look beyond the facts and information to what the writer really wants to say about his or her subject, you're looking for the main idea.

One of the most common questions on reading comprehension exams is, "What is the main idea of this passage?" How would you answer this question for the paragraph below?

> "Wilma Rudolph, the crippled child who became an Olympic running champion, is an inspiration for us all. Born prematurely in 1940, Wilma spent her childhood battling illness, including measles, scarlet fever, chicken pox, pneumonia, and polio, a crippling disease which at that time had no cure. At the age of four, she was told she would never walk again. But Wilma and her family refused to give up. After years of special treatment and physical therapy, 12-year-old Wilma was able to walk normally again. But walking wasn't enough for Wilma, who was determined to be an athlete. Before long, her talent earned her a spot in the 1956 Olympics, where she earned a bronze medal. In the 1960 Olympics, the height of her career, she won three gold medals."

What is the main idea of this paragraph? You might be tempted to answer, "Wilma Rudolph" or "Wilma Rudolph's life." Yes, Wilma Rudolph's life is the **subject** of the passage—who or what the passage is about—but the subject is not necessarily the main idea. The **main idea** is what the writer wants to say about this subject. What is the main thing the writer says about Wilma's life?

Which of the following statements is the main idea of the paragraph?
- a) Wilma Rudolph was very sick as a child.
- b) Wilma Rudolph was an Olympic champion.
- c) Wilma Rudolph is someone to admire.

Main idea: The overall fact, feeling, or thought a writer wants to convey about his or her subject.

The best answer is **c)**: Wilma Rudolph is someone to admire. This is the idea the paragraph adds up to; it's what holds all of the information in the paragraph together. This example also shows two important characteristics of a main idea:

1. It is **general** enough to encompass all of the ideas in the passage.

2. It is an **assertion.** An assertion is a statement made by the writer.

The main idea of a passage must be general enough to encompass all of the ideas in the passage. It should be broad enough for all of the other sentences in that passage to fit underneath it, like people under an umbrella. Notice that the first two options, "Wilma Rudolph was very sick as a child" and "Wilma Rudolph was an Olympic champion", are too specific to be the main idea. They aren't broad enough to cover all of the ideas in the passage, because the passage talks about both her illnesses and her Olympic achievements. Only the third answer is general enough to be the main idea of the paragraph.

A main idea is also some kind of **assertion** about the subject. An assertion is a claim that something is true. Assertions can be facts or opinions, but in either case, an assertion should be supported by specific ideas, facts, and details. In other words, the main idea makes a general assertion that tells readers that something is true.

The supporting sentences, on the other hand, show readers that this assertion is true by providing specific facts and details. For example, in the Wilma Rudolph paragraph, the writer makes a general assertion: "Wilma Rudolph, the crippled child who became an Olympic running champion, is an inspiration for us all." The other sentences offer specific facts and details that prove why Wilma Rudolph is an inspirational person.

Writers often state their main ideas in one or two sentences so that readers can have a very clear understanding about the main point of the passage. A sentence that expresses the main idea of a paragraph is called a **topic sentence.**

Notice, for example, how the first sentence in the Wilma Rudolph paragraph states the main idea:

"Wilma Rudolph, the crippled child who became an Olympic running champion, is an inspiration for us all."

This sentence is therefore the topic sentence for the paragraph. Topic sentences are often found at the beginning of paragraphs. Sometimes, though, writers begin with specific supporting ideas and lead up to the main idea, and in this case the topic sentence is often found at the end of the paragraph. Sometimes the topic sentence is even found somewhere in the middle, and other times there isn't a clear topic sentence at all—but that doesn't mean there isn't a main idea; the author has just chosen not to express it in a clear topic sentence. In this last case, you'll have to look carefully at the paragraph for clues about the main idea.

Main Ideas vs. Supporting Ideas

If you're not sure whether something is a main idea or a supporting idea, ask yourself the following question: is the sentence making a **general statement,** or is it providing **specific information?** In the Wilma Rudolph paragraph above, for example, all of the sentences except the first make specific statements. They are not general enough to serve as an umbrella or net for the whole paragraph.

Writers often provide clues that can help you distinguish between main ideas and their supporting ideas. Here are some of the most common words and phrases used to introduce specific examples:

1. **For example…**

2. **Specifically…**

3. **In addition…**

4. **Furthermore…**

5. **For instance…**

6. **Others…**

7. **In particular…**

8. **Some…**

These signal words tell you that a supporting fact or idea will follow. If you're having trouble finding the main idea of a paragraph, try climinating sentences that begin with these phrases, because they will most likely be too specific to be a main ideas.

Implied Main Idea

When the main idea is **implied**, there's no topic sentence, which means that finding the main idea requires some detective work. But don't worry! You already know the importance of structure, word choice, style, and tone. Plus, you know how to read carefully to find clues, and you know that these clues will help you figure out the main idea.

For Example:

"One of my summer reading books was *The Windows of Time*. Though it's more than 100 pages long, I read it in one afternoon. I couldn't wait to see what happened to Evelyn, the main character. But by the time I got to the end, I wondered if I should have spent my afternoon doing something else. The ending was so awful that I completely forgot that I'd enjoyed most of the book."

There's no topic sentence here, but you should still be able to find the main idea. Look carefully at what the writer says and how she says it. What is she suggesting?

    a) *The Windows of Time* is a terrific novel.
    b) *The Windows of Time* is disappointing.
    c) *The Windows of Time* is full of suspense.
    d) *The Windows of Time* is a lousy novel.

The correct answer is **b)** – the novel is disappointing. How can you tell that this is the main idea? First, we can eliminate choice **c)**, because it's too specific to be a main idea. It deals only with one specific aspect of the novel (its suspense).

Sentences **a)**, **b)**, and **d)**, on the other hand, all express a larger idea – a general assertion about the quality of the novel. But only one of these statements can actually serve as a "net" for the whole paragraph. Notice that while the first few sentences praise the novel, the last two criticize it. Clearly, this is a mixed review.

Therefore, the best answer is **b)**. Sentence **a)** is too positive and doesn't account for the "awful" ending. Sentence **d)**, on the other hand, is too negative and doesn't account for the reader's sense of suspense and interest in the main character. But sentence **b)** allows for both positive and negative aspects – when a good thing turns bad, we often feel disappointed.

Now let's look at another example. Here, the word choice will be more important, so read carefully.

> "Fortunately, none of Toby's friends had ever seen the apartment where Toby lived with his mother and sister. Sandwiched between two burnt-out buildings, his two-story apartment building was by far the ugliest one on the block. It was a real eyesore: peeling orange paint (orange!), broken windows, crooked steps, crooked everything. He could just imagine what his friends would say if they ever saw this poor excuse for a building."

Which of the following expresses the main idea of this paragraph?

    a) Toby wishes he could move to a nicer building.
    b) Toby wishes his dad still lived with them.
    c) Toby is glad none of his friends know where he lives.
    d) Toby is sad because he doesn't have any friends.

From the description, we can safely assume that Toby doesn't like his apartment building and wishes he could move to a nicer building **a)**. But that idea isn't general enough to cover the whole paragraph, because it's about his building.

Because the first sentence states that Toby has friends, the answer cannot be **d)**. We know that Toby lives only with his mother and little sister, so we might assume that he wishes his dad still lived with them, **b)**, but there's nothing in the paragraph to support that assumption, and this idea doesn't include the two main topics of the paragraph—Toby's building and Toby's friends.

What the paragraph adds up to is that Toby is terribly embarrassed about his building, and he's glad that none of his friends have seen it **c)**. This is the main idea. The paragraph opens with the word "fortunately," so we know that he thinks it's a good thing none of his friends have been to his house. Plus, notice how the building is described: "by far the ugliest on the block," which says a lot since it's stuck "between two burnt-out buildings." The writer calls it an "eyesore," and repeats "orange" with an exclamation point to emphasize how ugly the color is. Everything is "crooked" in this "poor excuse for a building." Toby is clearly ashamed of where he lives and worries about what his friends would think if they saw it.

Cause and Effect

Understanding cause and effect is important for reading success. Every event has at least one cause (what made it happen) and at least one effect (the result of what happened). Some events have more than one cause, and some have more than one effect. An event is also often part of a chain of causes and effects. Causes and effects are usually signaled by important transitional words and phrases.

Words Indicating Cause:

1. **Because (of)**

2. **Created (by)**

3. **Caused (by)**

4. **Since**

Words Indicating Effect:

1. **As a result**

2. **Since**

3. **Consequently**

4. **So**

5. **Hence**

6. **Therefore**

Sometimes, a writer will offer his or her opinion about why an event happened when the facts of the cause(s) aren't clear. Or a writer may predict what he or she thinks will happen because of a certain event (its effects). If this is the case, you need to consider how reasonable those opinions are. Are the writer's ideas logical? Does the writer offer support for the conclusions he or she offers?

Reading Between the Lines

Paying attention to word choice is particularly important when the main idea of a passage isn't clear. A writer's word choice doesn't just affect meaning; it also creates it. For example, look at the following description from a teacher's evaluation of a student applying to a special foreign language summer camp. There's no topic sentence, but if you use your powers of observation, you should be able to tell how the writer feels about her subject.

> "As a student, Jane usually completes her work on time and checks it carefully. She speaks French well and is learning to speak with less of an American accent. She has often been a big help to other students who are just beginning to learn the language."

What message does this passage send about Jane? Is she the best French student the writer has ever had? Is she one of the worst, or is she just average? To answer these questions, you have to make an inference, and you must support your inference with specific observations. What makes you come to the conclusion that you come to?

The **diction** of the paragraph above reveals that this is a positive evaluation, but not a glowing recommendation. Here are some of the specific observations you might have made to support this conclusion:

- The writer uses the word "usually" in the first sentence. This means that Jane is good about meeting deadlines for work, but not great; she doesn't always hand in her work on time.

- The first sentence also says that Jane checks her work carefully. While Jane may sometimes hand in work late, at least she always makes sure it's quality work. She's not sloppy.

- The second sentence tells us she's "learning to speak with less of an American accent." This suggests that she has a strong accent and needs to improve in this area. It also suggests, though, that she is already making progress.

- The third sentence tells us that she "often" helps "students who are just beginning to learn the language." From this we can conclude that Jane has indeed mastered the basics. Otherwise, how could she be a big help to students who are just starting to learn? By looking at the passage carefully, then, you can see how the writer feels about her subject.

VOCABULARY

You may also be asked to provide definitions or intended meanings for words within passages. Some of those words, you may never have encountered before the test. But there are ways to answer correctly, and confidently, regardless!

Context Clues

The most fundamental vocabulary skill is using the context of a word to determine its meaning. Your ability to observe sentences closely is extremely useful when it comes to understanding new vocabulary words.

Types of Context

There are two different types of context that can help you understand the meaning of unfamiliar words: **sentence context** and **situational context**. Regardless of which context is present, these types of questions are not really testing your knowledge of vocabulary; rather, they test your ability to comprehend the meaning of a word through its usage.

Situational context is context that comes from understanding the situation in which a word or phrase occurs.

Sentence context occurs within the sentence that contains the vocabulary word. To figure out words using sentence context clues, you should first determine the most important words in the sentence.

Example: I had a hard time reading her <u>illegible</u> handwriting.
a) Neat.
b) Unsafe.
c) Sloppy.
d) Educated.

Already, you know that this sentence is discussing something that is hard to read. Look at the word that **illegible** is describing: **handwriting**. Based on context clues, you can tell that illegible means that her handwriting is hard to read.

Next, look at the answer choices. Choice **a) Neat** is obviously a wrong answer because neat handwriting would not be difficult to read. Choice **b) Unsafe** and **d) Educated** don't make sense. Therefore, choice **c) Sloppy** is the best answer choice.

Types of Clues
There are four types of clues that can help you understand context, and therefore the meaning of a word. They are **restatement**, **positive/negative**, **contrast**, and **specific detail**.

Restatement clues occur when the definition of the word is clearly stated in the sentence.

> **Example**: The dog was <u>dauntless</u> in the face of danger, braving the fire to save the girl.
> a) Difficult.
> b) Fearless.
> c) Imaginative.

Demonstrating **bravery** in the face of danger would be **fearless,** choice **b)**. In this case, the context clues tell you exactly what the word means.

Positive/negative clues can tell you whether a word has a positive or negative meaning.

> **Example**: The magazine gave a great review of the fashion show, stating the clothing was **sublime**.
> a) Horrible.
> b) Exotic.
> c) Bland
> d) Gorgeous.

The sentence tells us that the author liked the clothing enough to write a **great** review, so you know that the best answer choice is going to be a positive word. Therefore, you can immediately rule out choices **a)** and **c)** because they are negative words. **Exotic** is a neutral word; alone, it doesn't inspire a **great** review. The most positive word is gorgeous, which makes choice **d) Gorgeous** the best answer.

The following sentence uses both restatement and positive/negative clues:

> "Janet suddenly found herself <u>destitute</u>, so poor she could barely afford to eat."

The second part of the sentence clearly indicates that destitute is a negative word; it also restates the meaning: very poor.

Contrast clues include the opposite meaning of a word. Words like **but, on the other hand**, and **however** are tip-offs that a sentence contains a contrast clue.

> **Example**: Beth did not spend any time preparing for the test, but Tyron kept a <u>rigorous</u> study schedule.
> a) Strict.
> b) Loose.
> c) Boring.
> d) Strange.

In this case, the word **but** tells us that Tyron studied in a different way than Beth. If Beth did not study very hard, then Tyron did study hard for the test. The best answer here, therefore, is choice **a) Strict**.

Specific detail clues give a precise detail that can help you understand the meaning of the word.

> **Example**: The box was heavier than he expected and it began to become <u>cumbersome</u>.
> a) Impossible.
> b) Burdensome.
> c) Obligated.
> d) Easier.

Start by looking at the specific details of the sentence. Choice **d)** can be eliminated right away because it is doubtful it would become **easier** to carry something that is **heavier**. There are also no clues in the sentence to indicate he was **obligated** to carry the box, so choice **c)** can also be disregarded. The sentence specifics, however, do tell you that the package was cumbersome because it was heavy to carry; this is a burden, which is **burdensome**, choice **b)**.

It is important to remember that more than one of these clues can be present in the same sentence. The more there are, the easier it will be to determine the meaning of the word, so look for them.

Denotation and Connotation

As you know, many English words have more than one meaning. For example, the word **quack** has two distinct definitions: the sound a duck makes; and a person who publicly pretends to have a skill, knowledge, education, or qualification which they do not possess.

The **denotations** of a word are the dictionary definitions.

The **connotations** of a word are the implied meaning(s) or emotion which the word makes you think.

> **Example**: "Sure," Pam said excitedly, "I'd just love to join your club; it sounds so exciting!"

Now, read this sentence:

"Sure," Pam said sarcastically, "I'd just love to join your club; it sounds so exciting!"

Even though the two sentences only differ by one word, they have completely different meanings. The difference, of course, lies in the words "excitedly" and "sarcastically."

Prefixes, Roots, and Suffixes

Although you are not expected to know every word in the English language for your test, you will need to have the ability to use deductive reasoning to find the choice that is the best match for the word in question, which is why we are going to explain how to break a word into its parts of meaning.

prefix – root – suffix

One trick in dividing a word into its parts is to first divide the word into its **syllables**. To show how syllables can help you find roots and affixes, we'll use the word **descendant,** which means one who comes from an ancestor. Start by dividing the word into its individual syllables; this word has three:

de-scend-ant.

The next step is to look at the beginning and end of the word, and then determine if these syllables are prefixes, suffixes, or possible roots. You can then use the meanings of each part to guide you in defining the word. When you divide words into their specific parts, they do not always add up to an exact definition, but you will see a relationship between their parts.

Note: This trick won't always work in every situation, because not all prefixes, roots, and suffixes have only one syllable. For example, take the word **monosyllabic** (which ironically means "one syllable"). There are five syllables in that word, but only three parts. The prefix is "mono," meaning "one." The root "syllab" refers to "syllable," while the suffix "ic" means "pertaining to." Therefore, we have – very ironically – one extremely long word which means "pertaining to one syllable."

Roots
Roots are the building blocks of all words. Every word is either a root itself or has a root. Just as a plant cannot grow without roots, neither can vocabulary, because a word must have a root to give it meaning.

       Example: The test instructions were **unclear.**

The root is what is left when you strip away all the prefixes and suffixes from a word. In this case, take away the prefix "un-," and you have the root **clear.**

Roots are not always recognizable words, because they generally come from Latin or Greek words, such as **nat**, a Latin root meaning **born.** The word native, which means a person born of a referenced placed, comes from this root, so does the word prenatal, meaning before birth. Yet, if you used the prefix **nat** instead of born, just on its own, no one would know what you were talking about.

Words can also have more than one root. For example, the word **omnipoten**t means all powerful. Omnipotent is a combination of the roots **omni-**, meaning all or every, and **-potent**, meaning power or strength. In this case, **omni** cannot be used on its own as a single word, but **potent** can.

Again, it is important to keep in mind that roots do not always match the exact definitions of words and they can have several different spellings, but breaking a word into its parts is still one of the best ways to determine its meaning.

Prefixes
Prefixes are syllables added to the beginning of a word and suffixes are syllables added to the end of the word. Both carry assigned meanings. The common name for prefixes and suffixes is **affixes**. Affixes do not have to be attached directly to a root and a word can often have more than one prefix and/or suffix.

Prefixes and suffixes can be attached to a word to completely change the word's meaning or to enhance the word's original meaning. Although they don't mean much to us on their own, when attached to other words affixes can make a world of difference.

Let's use the word **prefix** itself as an example:

Fix means to place something securely; and **Pre** means before. Therefore, **Prefix** means to place something before or in front.

Suffixes
Suffixes come after the root of a word.

Example: Feminism.

Femin is a root. It means female, woman. **-ism** means act, practice or process. **Feminism** is the defining and establishing of equal political, economic, and social rights for women.

Unlike prefixes, **suffixes** can be used to change a word's part of speech.

Example: "Randy raced to the finish line." VS "Shana's costume was very racy."

In the first sentence, raced is a verb. In the second sentence, racy is an adjective. By changing the suffix from **-ed** to **-y**, the word race changes from a verb into an adjective, which has an entirely different meaning.

Although you cannot determine the meaning of a word by a prefix or suffix alone, you *can* use your knowledge of what root words mean to eliminate answer choices; indicating if the word is positive or negative can give you a partial meaning of the word.

Test Your Knowledge: Language Arts – The Reading Section

Questions 1 – 4 are based on the following passage:

From *"On Lying Awake at Night"* by Stewart Edward White (public domain):

About once in so often you are due to lie awake at night. Why this is so I have never been able to discover. It apparently comes from no predisposing uneasiness of indigestion, no rashness in the matter of too much tea or tobacco, no excitation of unusual incident or stimulating conversation. In fact, you turn in with the expectation of rather a good night's rest. Almost at once the little noises of the forest grow larger, blend in the hollow bigness of the first drowse; your thoughts drift idly back and forth between reality and dream; when—*snap!*—you are broad awake!

For, unlike mere insomnia, lying awake at night in the woods is pleasant. The eager, nervous straining for sleep gives way to a delicious indifference. You do not care. Your mind is cradled in an exquisite poppy-suspension of judgment and of thought. Impressions slip vaguely into your consciousness and as vaguely out again. Sometimes they stand stark and naked for your inspection; sometimes they lose themselves in the mist of half-sleep. Always they lay soft velvet fingers on the drowsy imagination, so that in their caressing you feel the vaster spaces from which they have come. Peaceful-brooding your *faculties* receive. Hearing, sight, smell—all are preternaturally keen to whatever of sound and sight and woods perfume is abroad through the night; and yet at the same time active appreciation dozes, so these things lie on it sweet and cloying like fallen rose-leaves.

Nothing is more fantastically unreal to tell about, nothing more concretely real to experience, than this undernote of the quick water. And when you do lie awake at night, it is always making its unobtrusive appeal. Gradually its hypnotic spell works. The distant chimes ring louder and nearer as you cross the borderland of sleep. And then outside the tent some little woods noise snaps the thread. An owl hoots, a whippoorwill cries, a twig cracks beneath the cautious prowl of some night creature—at once the yellow sunlit French meadows puff away—you are staring at the blurred image of the moon spraying through the texture of your tent.

(You have cast from you with the warm blanket the drowsiness of dreams. A coolness, physical and spiritual, bathes you from head to foot. All your senses are keyed to the last vibrations. You hear the littler night prowlers; you glimpse the greater. A faint, searching woods perfume of dampness greets your nostrils. And somehow, mysteriously, in a manner not to be understood, the forces of the world seem in suspense, as though a touch might crystallize infinite possibilities into infinite power and motion. But the touch lacks. The forces hover on the edge of action, unheeding the little noises. In all humbleness and awe, you are a dweller of the Silent Places.

The night wind from the river, or from the open spaces of the wilds, chills you after a time. You begin to think of your blankets. In a few moments you roll yourself in their soft wool. Instantly it is morning.

And, strange to say, you have not to pay by going through the day unrefreshed. You may feel like turning in at eight instead of nine, and you may fall asleep with unusual promptitude, but your journey will begin clear-headedly, proceed springily, and end with much in reserve. No languor, no dull headache, no exhaustion, follows your experience. For this once your two hours of sleep have been as effective as nine.

1. In Paragraph 2, "faculties" is used to mean:
     a) Teachers.
     b) Senses.
     c) Imaginations.
     d) Capacities.

2. The author's opinion of insomnia is that:
     a) It is not a problem because nights without sleep are refreshing.
     b) It can happen more often when sleeping in the woods because of the noises in nature.
     c) It is generally unpleasant, but sometimes can be hypnotic.
     d) It is the best way to cultivate imagination.

3. By "strange to say" in Paragraph 6, the author means:
     a) The experience of the night before had an unreal quality.
     b) The language used in describing the night before is not easily understood.
     c) It is not considered acceptable to express the opinion the author expresses.
     d) Contrary to expectations, one is well-rested after the night before.

4. How is this essay best characterized?
     a) A playful examination of a common medical problem.
     b) A curious look at both sides of an issue.
     c) A fanciful description of the author's experience.
     d) A horrific depiction of night hallucinations.

Questions 5-10 are based on the following passages:

Passage One
An excerpt from the essay *"Tradition and the Individual Talent"* by T.S. Eliot (public domain):

No poet, no artist of any art, has his complete meaning alone. His significance, his appreciation is the appreciation of his relation to the dead poets and artists. You cannot value him alone; you must set him, for contrast and comparison, among the dead. I mean this as a principle of aesthetic, not merely historical, criticism. The necessity that he shall conform, that he shall cohere, is not one-sided; what happens when a new work of art is created is something that happens simultaneously to all the works of art which preceded it. The existing monuments form an ideal order among themselves, which is modified by the introduction of the new (the really new) work of art among them. The existing order is complete before the new work arrives; for order to persist after the supervention of novelty, the *whole* existing order must be, if ever so slightly, altered; and so the relations, proportions, values of each work of art toward the whole are readjusted; and this is conformity between the old and the new. Whoever has approved this idea of order, of the form of European, of English literature, will not find it preposterous that the past should be altered by the present as much as the present is directed by the past. And the poet who is aware of this will be aware of great difficulties and responsibilities.

Passage Two
An excerpt from the Clive Bell's seminal art history book *"Art"* (public domain):

To criticize a work of art historically is to play the science-besotted fool. No more disastrous theory ever issued from the brain of a charlatan than that of evolution in art. Giotto[1] did not creep, a grub, that Titian[2] might flaunt, a butterfly. To think of a man's art as leading on to the art of someone else is to misunderstand it. To praise or abuse or be interested in a work of art because it leads or does not lead to another work of art is to treat it as though it were not a work of art. The connection of one work of art with another may have everything to do with history: it has nothing to do with appreciation. So soon as we begin to consider a work as anything else than an end in itself we leave the world of art. Though the development of painting from Giotto to Titian may be interesting historically, it cannot affect the value of any particular picture: aesthetically, it is of no consequence whatever. Every work of art must be judged on its own merits.

5. In Passage One, the word "cohere" is used to most closely mean:
   a) To be congruous with.
   b) To supplant.
   c) To imitate.
   d) To overhaul.
   e) To deviate from.

6. In Passage Two, the author alludes to a butterfly to contradict which concept?
   a) The theory of evolution is responsible for the discipline of art criticism.
   b) Scientific knowledge is not necessary to understand paintings.
   c) Artists who show off are doomed to be criticized.
   d) Art which finds inspiration in nature is the highest form of art.
   e) Titian's art is beautiful as a result of the horrible art that came before.

7. The author of Passage One would be most likely to support:
   a) An artist who imitated the great works of the past.
   b) An art critic who relied solely on evaluating the aesthetics of new art.
   c) A historian who studied the aesthetic evolution of art.
   d) An artist who was also a scientist.
   e) An artist who shouldered the burden of creating something new, while affecting the old, in the world of art.

8. The meaning of the sentence "To praise or abuse or be interested in a work of art because it leads or does not lead to another work of art is to treat it as though it were not a work of art" in Passage 2 means:
   a) Works of art cannot be judged primarily by their relation to one another.
   b) One should not vandalize works of art.
   c) It is necessary to understand how one work of art leads to another in order to judge it.
   d) Works of art must be treated with respect.
   e) Understanding works of art is reliant on seeing them on a historical scale.

---

[1] Giotto was an Italian painter during the Middle Ages.
[2] Titian was an Italian painter during the Renaissance.

9. The author of Passage One would likely agree with which of the following statements?
   a) The past is a monument that is unalterable by the present.
   b) Historical knowledge is entirely separate from artistic knowledge.
   c) To understand a novel written in the twentieth century, it is necessary to have some knowledge of nineteenth century literature.
   d) Painters of Italian descent are all related to one another.
   e) One cannot be a scholar of literary history without also being a scholar of scientific thought.

10. The authors of both passages would likely agree with which of the following statements?
   a) An aesthetic judgment is the greatest possible approach to art criticism.
   b) Knowledge of history compromises one's ability to criticize works of art.
   c) The painter Titian was able to create his art as a consequence of the art which came before his time.
   d) It is imperative to understand the progression from one work of art to another.
   e) Not all works of art are consequential.

Questions 11 and 12 are based on the following passage:

Excerpt from Anne Walker's "*A Matter of Proportion*," a short science-fiction story published in 1959 (public domain). In this excerpt, one character tells another about an injured man who is planning a secret operation:

On the way, he filled in background. Scott had been living out of the hospital in a small apartment, enjoying as much liberty as he could manage. He had equipment so he could stump around, and an antique car specially equipped. He wasn't complimentary about them. Orthopedic products had to be: unreliable, hard to service, unsightly, intricate, and uncomfortable. If they also squeaked and cut your clothes, fine!

Having to plan every move with an eye on weather and a dozen other factors, he developed an uncanny foresight. Yet he had to improvise at a moment's notice. With life a continuous high-wire act, he trained every surviving fiber to precision, dexterity, and tenacity. Finally, he avoided help. Not pride, self-preservation; the compulsively helpful have rarely the wit to ask before rushing in to knock you on your face, so he learned to bide his time till the horizon was clear of beaming simpletons. Also, he found an interest in how far he could go.

11. Why does Scott primarily avoid the help of others?
   a) He has found that he is usually better off without it.
   b) He does not want to rely on other people for anything.
   c) He is doing experiments to test his own limits.
   d) He is working on a secret operation and cannot risk discovery.
   e) He does not realize that he needs assistance.

12. "Orthopedic" in paragraph one most nearly means:
- a) Uncomfortable.
- b) Dangerous.
- c) Corrective.
- d) Enhanced.
- e) Complicated.

Questions 13 – 18 are based on the following passage:

Excerpt from Rennie W. Doane's *"Insects and Disease,"* a popular science account published in 1910 (public domain):

It has been estimated that there are about four thousand species or kinds of Protozoans, about twenty-five thousand species of Mollusks, about ten thousand species of birds, about three thousand five hundred species of mammals, and from two hundred thousand to one million species of insects, or from two to five times as many kinds of insects as all other animals combined.

Not only do the insects preponderate in number of species, but the number of individuals belonging to many of the species is absolutely beyond our comprehension. Try to count the number of little green aphis on a single infested rose-bush, or on a cabbage plant; guess at the number of mosquitoes issuing each day from a good breeding-pond; estimate the number of scale insects on a single square inch of a tree badly infested with San José scale; then try to think how many more bushes or trees or ponds may be breeding their millions just as these and you will only begin to comprehend the meaning of this statement.

As long as these myriads of insects keep, in what we are pleased to call their proper place, we care not for their numbers and think little of them except as some student points out some wonderful thing about their structure, life-history or adaptations. But since the dawn of history we find accounts to show that insects have not always kept to their proper sphere but have insisted at various times and in various ways in interfering with man's plans and wishes, and on account of their excessive numbers the results have often been most disastrous.

Insects cause an annual loss to the people of the United States of over $1,000,000,000. Grain fields are devastated; orchards and gardens are destroyed or seriously affected; forests are made waste places and in scores of other ways these little pests which do not keep in their proper places are exacting this tremendous tax from our people. These things have been known and recognized for centuries, and scores of volumes have been written about the insects and their ways and of methods of combating them.

Yellow fever, while not so widespread as malaria, is more fatal and therefore more terrorizing. Its presence and spread are due entirely to a single species of mosquito, *Stegomyia calopus*. While this species is usually restricted to tropical or semi-tropical regions it sometimes makes its appearance in places farther north, especially in summer time, where it may thrive for a time. The adult mosquito is black, conspicuously marked with white. The legs and abdomen are banded with white and on the thorax is a series of white lines which in well-preserved specimens distinctly resembles a lyre. These mosquitoes are essentially domestic insects, for they are very rarely found except in houses or in their immediate vicinity. Once they enter a room they will scarcely leave it except to lay their eggs in a near-by cistern, water-pot, or some other convenient place.

Their habit of biting in the daytime has gained for them the name of "day mosquitoes" to distinguish them from the night feeders. But they will bite at night as well as by day and many other species are not at all adverse to a daylight meal, if the opportunity offers, so this habit is not distinctive. The recognition of these facts has a distinct bearing in the methods adopted to prevent the spread of yellow fever. There are no striking characters or habits in the larval or pupal stages that would enable us to distinguish without careful examination this species from other similar forms with which it might be associated. For some time it was claimed that this species would breed only in clean water, but it has been found that it is not nearly so particular, some even claiming that it prefers foul water. I have seen them breeding in countless thousands in company with *Stegomyia scutellaris* and *Culex fatigans* in the sewer drains in Tahiti in the streets of Papeete. As the larva feed largely on bacteria one would expect to find them in exactly such places where the bacteria are of course abundant. The fact that they are able to live in any kind of water and in a very small amount of it well adapts them to their habits of living about dwellings.

13. Why does the author list the amounts of different species of organisms in paragraph 1?
   a) To illustrate the vast number of species in the world.
   b) To demonstrate authority on the subject of insects.
   c) To establish the relative importance of mollusks and birds.
   d) To demonstrate the proportion of insects to other organisms.

14. What does the author use "their proper place" at the beginning of paragraph 3?
   a) The author is alluding to people's tendency to view insects as largely irrelevant to their lives.
   b) The author feels that insects belong only outdoors.
   c) The author wants the reader to feel superior to insects.
   d) The author is warning that insects can evolve to affect the course of human events.

15. This passage can be characterized primarily as:
   a) Pedantic.
   b) Droll.
   c) Informative.
   d) Abstract.
   e) Cautionary.

16. The main idea of this passage is best summarized as:
   a) Disease-carrying mosquitoes have adapted to best live near human settlements.
   b) Insects can have a detrimental effect on the economy by destroying crops.
   c) Insects are numerous in both types of species and individuals within a species.
   d) Although people do not always consider insects consequential, they can have substantial effects on human populations.

17. The use of "domestic" in Paragraph 5 most nearly means:
   a) Originating in the United States.
   b) Under the care of and bred by humans.
   c) Fearful of the outdoors.
   d) Living near human homes.

18. Which of the following ideas would best belong in this passage?

    a) An historical example of the effect a yellow fever outbreak had on civilization.

    b) A biological explanation of how diseases are transmitted from insects to humans.

    c) A reference to the numbers of insects which live far away from human habitation.

    d) Strategies for the prevention of yellow fever and malaria.

Questions 19 – 26 are based on a long original passage (author Elissa Yeates):

The collapse of the arbitrage[3] firm Long-Term Capital Management (LTCM) in 1998 is explained by a host of different factors: its investments were based on a high level of leverage, for example, and it was significantly impacted by Russia's default on the ruble. However, sociologist Donald MacKenzie maintains that the main factor in LTCM's demise was that, like all arbitrage firms, it was subjected to the sociological phenomena of the arbitrage community; namely, imitation. Arbitrageurs, who are generally known to one another as members of a specific subset of the financial society, use decision-making strategies based not only on mathematical models or pure textbook reason, but also based upon their feelings and gut reactions toward the financial market and on the actions of their peers. This imitation strategy leads to the overlapping "super portfolio," which creates an inherent instability that leads to collapse, the most infamous example being LTCM.

The public opinion of the partners of the firm in 1998 was that it had acted cavalierly with borrowed capital. However, in actuality the firm's strategy was exceedingly conservative, with a diversified portfolio, overestimated risks, and carefully hedged investments. The firm even tested tactics for dealing with financial emergencies such as the collapse of the European Monetary Union. Before the 1998 crisis, those in LTCM were never accused of recklessness. Nor were they, as is sometimes explained, overly reliant on mathematical models. The statistical hubris explanation falters under MacKenzie's evidence that John Meriwether and the others who ran the firm made their investment decisions based more upon their intricate understandings of the arbitrage market rather than upon the pure results of mathematical analyses. The financial instability that was created was not the result of the decision-making of one firm; but rather, the collective patterns of decision-making of all of the arbitrage firms at the time.

The infamy of LTCM worked against the company. LTCM was composed of some of the most eminent minds in finance and it made devastating profits for the first few years that it was running. This led to imitation by other arbitrageurs who viewed the investments of LTCM as nearly sure bets. This type of replication of investment portfolios is not surprising, considering that arbitrageurs are all looking for similar types of pricing discrepancies and anomalies to exploit. The structure of arbitrageurs as a unique subset of the financial community who are largely personally known to one another further contributes to this phenomenon. Because of these factors over time the various players in the field of arbitrage created overlapping investments which MacKenzie dubs a "super portfolio." While LTCM alone may have created a geographically and industrially diverse portfolio, across the discipline of arbitrage as a whole capital flocked to similar investments.

Because of this super portfolio trend, multiple arbitrageurs were affected by the price changes of different assets caused by the actions of single independent firms. MacKenzie cites the example of the

---

[3] "Arbitrage" is a financial strategy which takes advantage of the temporary price differences of a single asset in different markets.

takeover of the investment bank Salomon Brothers by the Travelers Corporation. Salomon Brothers' portfolio, now under the management of someone who disliked the risks of arbitrage trading, liquidated its positions, which drove down the prices of assets in the markets in which it operated. The liquidation of the holdings of such a prominent player in the arbitrage game negatively affected the positions of every other firm that had a stake in those markets, including, of course, LTCM. This also illustrates the other sociological side of MacKenzie's argument: that arbitrageurs are subject to irrational internal pressures to cut their losses before their investments play out, which one of his interview subjects terms "queasiness" when faced with a stretch of losses.

19. The second paragraph of this passage primarily aims to:
    a) Explain that recklessness with borrowed capital is never profitable.
    b) Explore the factors ultimately responsible for the demise of the arbitrage firm Long-Term Capital Management.
    c) Demonstrate how the practice of arbitrage works.
    d) Laud the use of statistical models in calculating financial risks.
    e) Present and dismiss several theories of the collapse of Long-Term Capital Management.

20. In paragraph 2, "devastating" is used to mean:
    a) Destructive.
    b) Attractive.
    c) Blasphemous.
    d) Considerable.
    e) Appalling.

21. The final paragraph in this passage:
    a) Refutes the argument presented in the second paragraph of the passage.
    b) Gives a logical example of the phenomenon described in the introductory first paragraph of the passage.
    c) Contains an ardent plea against the passage of arbitrage.
    d) Gives a step-by-step account of the demise of Long-Term Capital Management.
    e) Argues that an understanding of sociology is crucial to successful financial practice.

22. Which of the following is a best description of the author's approach to the topic?
    a) Impassioned exposition.
    b) Curious exploration.
    c) Gleeful detection.
    d) Disgusted condemnation.
    e) Serene indifference.

23. Which of the following most accurately summarizes the author's thesis?
   a) If Long-Term Capital Management had developed a superportfolio, it would not have collapsed.
   b) Financial markets are inherently instable because those who participate in them are subject to human faults.
   c) Arbitrage firms should always endeavor to have geographically and industrially diverse investments.
   d) Long-Term Capital Management collapsed because arbitrageurs across the industry were investing in the same things, which caused instability.
   e) Long-Term Capital Management was run by financiers who were reckless and overly dependent on mathematical models, which is why it collapsed.

24. "Hubris" in paragraph 2 most likely means:
   a) Mathematical model.
   b) Reliance.
   c) Arrogance.
   d) Denial.
   e) Mistake.

25. Which of the following facts would undermine the main argument of the passage?
   a) The European Monetary Union was close to collapse in 1998.
   b) Some arbitrage firms steered clear of the practice of superportfolios.
   c) The Travelers Corporation was run by financiers who favored the practice of arbitrage.
   d) Arbitrageurs rarely communicate with one another or get information from the same source.
   e) Mathematical models used in finance in the 1990s were highly reliable.

26. Which of the following supports the argument made in the third paragraph?
   a) A detailed outline of the statistical models used by Long-Term Capital Management to make decisions.
   b) An explanation of how other arbitrage firms were able to learn the tactics practiced by Long-Term Capital Management.
   c) Examples of the differences between different investment portfolios of arbitrage firms.
   d) An outline of sociological theories about decision-making processes.
   e) A map showing the geographical diversity of arbitrage investors.

Questions 27 – 36 are based on a long passage excerpted from Robert Louis Stevenson's classic novel Treasure Island (public domain). In this passage, the narrator tells about an old sailor staying at his family's inn.

He had taken me aside one day and promised me a silver fourpenny on the first of every month if I would only keep my "weather-eye open for a seafaring man with one leg" and let him know the moment he appeared. Often enough when the first of the month came round and I applied to him for my wage, he would only blow through his nose at me and stare me down, but before the week was out he was sure to think better of it, bring me my fourpenny piece, and repeat his orders to look out for "the seafaring man with one leg."

How that personage haunted my dreams, I need scarcely tell you. On stormy nights, when the wind shook the four corners of the house and the surf roared along the cove and up the cliffs, I would see him in a thousand forms, and with a thousand diabolical expressions. Now the leg would be cut off at the knee, now at the hip; now he was a monstrous kind of a creature who had never had but the one leg, and that in the middle of his body. To see him leap and run and pursue me over hedge and ditch was the worst of nightmares. And altogether I paid pretty dear for my monthly fourpenny piece, in the shape of these abominable fancies.

But though I was so terrified by the idea of the seafaring man with one leg, I was far less afraid of the captain himself than anybody else who knew him. There were nights when he took a deal more rum and water than his head would carry; and then he would sometimes sit and sing his wicked, old, wild sea-songs, minding nobody; but sometimes he would call for glasses round and force all the trembling company to listen to his stories or bear a chorus to his singing. Often I have heard the house shaking with "Yo-ho-ho, and a bottle of rum," all the neighbors joining in for dear life, with the fear of death upon them, and each singing louder than the other to avoid remark. For in these fits he was the most overriding companion ever known; he would slap his hand on the table for silence all round; he would fly up in a passion of anger at a question, or sometimes because none was put, and so he judged the company was not following his story. Nor would he allow anyone to leave the inn till he had drunk himself sleepy and reeled off to bed.

His stories were what frightened people worst of all. Dreadful stories they were—about hanging, and walking the plank, and storms at sea, and the Dry Tortugas, and wild deeds and places on the Spanish Main. By his own account he must have lived his life among some of the wickedest men that God ever allowed upon the sea, and the language in which he told these stories shocked our plain country people almost as much as the crimes that he described. My father was always saying the inn would be ruined, for people would soon cease coming there to be tyrannized over and put down, and sent shivering to their beds; but I really believe his presence did us good. People were frightened at the time, but on looking back they rather liked it; it was a fine excitement in a quiet country life, and there was even a party of the younger men who pretended to admire him, calling him a "true sea-dog" and a "real old salt" and such like names, and saying there was the sort of man that made England terrible at sea.

In one way, indeed, he bade fair to ruin us, for he kept on staying week after week, and at last month after month, so that all the money had been long exhausted, and still my father never plucked up the heart to insist on having more. If ever he mentioned it, the captain blew through his nose so loudly that you might say he roared, and stared my poor father out of the room. I have seen him wringing his hands after such a rebuff, and I am sure the annoyance and the terror he lived in must have greatly hastened his early and unhappy death.

27. The purpose of Paragraph 3 is to:
    a) Illustrate how others view the captain.
    b) Explain the narrator's relationship with the captain.
    c) Give more background information about the inn where the narrator lives.
    d) Recount old seafaring lore.
    e) Explain why the captain is staying at this inn.

28. Which paragraph serves to evoke the life lived by sailors at sea?
    a) 1.
    b) 2.
    c) 3.
    d) 4.
    e) 5.

29. "Diabolical" in Paragraph 2 most nearly means:
    a) Angry.
    b) Judgmental.
    c) Contorted.
    d) Fiendish.
    e) Stoic.

30. What kind of character does the author reveal the captain to be the third paragraph?
    a) Temperamental.
    b) Generous.
    c) Jocund.
    d) Mysterious.
    e) Reserved.

31. What does the author reveal about the narrator in Paragraph 5?
    a) The narrator is afraid of the captain.
    b) The narrator is eager to go to sea.
    c) The narrator was often angry and annoyed.
    d) The narrator grew up in poverty.
    e) The narrator lost his father at an early age.

32. "Tyrannized" in Paragraph 4 is used to mean:
    a) Cajoled.
    b) Bullied.
    c) Frightened.
    d) Robbed.
    e) Ejected.

33. Which of the following statements about this passage is false?
    a) It is unclear whether the "seafaring man with one leg" actually exists.
    b) The narrator harbors a serious grudge against the captain.
    c) The narrator is interested in the captain's stories.
    d) The story takes place near the ocean.
    e) Most people who populate the story are afraid of the captain.

34. According to the captain, all of the following are hazards which can be encountered at sea EXCEPT:
    a) Hangings.
    b) Wicked men.
    c) Walking the plank.
    d) Storms.
    e) Sea monsters.

35. It can be inferred from the passage that:
    a) Singing was frowned upon in the community.
    b) The narrator never knew his mother.
    c) The narrator admired the captain.
    d) The captain is afraid of the seafaring man with one leg.
    e) The narrator went on to become a pirate.

36. By "they rather liked it" at the end of Paragraph 4, the author most closely means:
    a) The patrons of the inn enjoyed singing.
    b) The captain and others appreciated the rum available for sale at the inn.
    c) The narrator and his friends liked the stories the captain told.
    d) The captain provided entertainment at the inn, which would otherwise be boring.
    e) The narrator's parents liked having the captain around.

Questions 37 – 40 are based on a short passage excerpted from the introduction to **The Best American Humorous Short Stories**, *edited by Alexander Jessup (public domain).*

No book is duller than a book of jokes, for what is refreshing in small doses becomes nauseating when perused in large assignments. Humor in literature is at its best not when served merely by itself but when presented along with other ingredients of literary force in order to give a wide representation of life. Therefore "professional literary humorists," as they may be called, have not been much considered in making up this collection. In the history of American humor there are three names which stand out more prominently than all others before Mark Twain, who, however, also belongs to a wider classification: "Josh Billings" (Henry Wheeler Shaw, 1815-1885), "Petroleum V. Nasby" (David Ross Locke, 1833-1888), and "Artemus Ward" (Charles Farrar Browne, 1834-1867). In the history of American humor these names rank high; in the field of American literature and the American short story they do not rank so high. I have found nothing of theirs that was first-class both as humor and as short story. Perhaps just below these three should be mentioned George Horatio Derby (1823-1861), author of *Phoenixiana* (1855) and the *Squibob Papers* (1859), who wrote under the name "John Phoenix." As has been justly said, "Derby, Shaw, Locke and Browne carried to an extreme numerous tricks already invented by earlier American humorists, particularly the tricks of gigantic exaggeration and calm-faced mendacity, but they are plainly in the main channel of American humor, which had its origin in the first comments of settlers upon the conditions of the frontier, long drew its principal inspiration from the differences between that frontier and the more settled and compact regions of the country, and reached its highest development in Mark Twain, in his youth a child of the American frontier, admirer and imitator of Derby and Browne, and eventually a man of the world and one of its greatest humorists."

37. The author of this passage would disagree with all of the following statements EXCEPT:

    a) To be a successful storyteller, one must also be a professional literary humorist.

    b) Mark Twain is the most prominent American humorist.

    c) Lying with a straight face is a literary humorist device which had just been invented at the time this was published.

    d) The best joke books are the longest ones.

    e) Professional literary humorism is the highest form of writing.

38. The purpose of this passage is to:

    a) Scorn humorous writing as lesser than storytelling.

    b) Explain how writers use humorous literary devices.

    c) Provide contextual information about the landscape of American humorous writing.

    d) Make a case for the appreciation of the humorists Henry Shaw and David Locke.

    e) Deny the historical roots of American literary humor.

39. The word "prominently" in line four most closely means:

    a) Extravagantly.

    b) Inconspicuously.

    c) Significantly.

    d) Comically.

    e) Conceitedly.

40. Which of the following best summarizes the author's theory of the origins of American humorous writing?

    a) It started as a way of breaking away from British literary humor.

    b) It grew hand-in-hand with American storytelling.

    c) It was founded by Mark Twain.

    d) It was inspired by the differences between settlements and the frontier.

    e) It began with exaggerations and mendacity.

Test Your Knowledge: Language Arts – The Reading Section – Answers

1. b)
2. c)
3. e)
4. c)
5. a)
6. e)
7. e)
8. a)
9. c)
10. e)
11. a)
12. c)
13. d)
14. e)
15. c)
16. d)
17. e)
18. a)
19. e)
20. d)

21. b)
22. b)
23. d)
24. c)
25. d)
26. b)
27. a)
28. d)
29. d)
30. a)
31. e)
32. b)
33. b)
34. e)
35. c)
36. d)
37. b)
38. c)
39. c)
40. d)

Chapter 2: Language Arts – The Writing Section

The "Language Arts – Writing" section is divided into two parts: a series of multiple-choice questions which will test your knowledge of grammar, structure, and syntax; and an essay section wherein you will respond to a prompt given in order to demonstrate your writing capabilities. The two sections will be scored separately, and then those two scores will be combined together to give your overall writing section score. Our review has been similarly divided: We will first go over the multiple-choice section, as the skills which you learn there apply to the essay section as well.

PART ONE: THE MULTIPLE-CHOICE SECTION

There are three types of questions in the multiple-choice section of the writing test:

1. **Error Identification**: Tests your ability to recognize errors in sentence structure, grammar, and syntax.

2. **Sentence Improvement**: As the name suggests, you will be given choices to improve a presented sentence.

3. **Paragraph Improvement**: Tests your ability to revise sentences within a larger context.

You will have a total of 50 questions to answer with a 60 minute time limit.

Many of the concepts which you reviewed in the previous chapter are applicable to this chapter as well. There were, however, a few concepts which you'll need to know that were not covered in the previous chapter – we'll review them here.

Nouns, Pronouns, Verbs, Adjectives, and Adverbs

Nouns
Nouns are people, places, or things. They are typically the subject of a sentence. For example, "The hospital was very clean." The noun is "hospital;" it is the "place."

Pronouns
Pronouns essentially "replace" nouns. This allows a sentence to not sound repetitive. Take the sentence: "Sam stayed home from school because Sam was not feeling well." The word "Sam" appears twice in the same sentence. Instead, you can use a pronoun and say, "Sam stayed at home because *he* did not feel well." Sounds much better, right?

Most Common Pronouns:

- I, me, mine, my.

- You, your, yours.

- He, him, his.

- She, her, hers.

- It, its.

- We, us, our, ours.

- They, them, their, theirs.

Verbs
Remember the old commercial, "Verb: It's what you do"? That sums up verbs in a nutshell! Verbs are the "action" of a sentence; verbs "do" things.

They can, however, be quite tricky. Depending on the subject of a sentence, the tense of the word (past, present, future, etc.), and whether or not they are regular or irregular, verbs have many variations.

Example: "He runs to second base." The verb is "runs." This is a "regular verb."

Example: "I am 7 years old." The verb in this case is "am." This is an "irregular verb."

As mentioned, verbs must use the correct tense – and that tense must remain the same throughout the sentence. "I was baking cookies and eat some dough." That sounded strange, didn't it? That's because the two verbs "baking" and "eat" are presented in different tenses. "Was baking" occurred in the past; "eat," on the other hand, occurs in the present. Instead, it should be "**ate** some dough."

Adjectives
Adjectives are words that describe a noun and give more information. Take the sentence: "The boy hit the ball." If you want to know more about the noun "boy," then you could use an adjective to describe it.

"The **little** boy hit the ball." An adjective simply provides more information about a noun or subject in a sentence.

Adverb

For some reason, many people have a difficult time with adverbs – but don't worry! They are really quite simple. Adverbs are similar to adjectives in that they provide more information about a part of a sentence; however, they do **not** describe nouns – that's an adjective's job. Instead, adverbs describe verbs, adjectives, and even other adverbs.

Take the sentence: "The doctor said she hired a new employee."

It would give more information to say: "The doctor said she **recently** hired a new employee." Now we know more about *how* the action was executed. Adverbs typically describe when or how something has happened, how it looks, how it feels, etc.

> **Good vs. Well**
>
> A very common mistake that people make concerning adverbs is the misuse of the word "good."
>
> "Good" is an adjective – things taste good, look good, and smell good. "Good" can even be a noun – "Superman does good" – when the word is speaking about "good" vs. "evil." HOWEVER, "good" is never an adverb.
>
> People commonly say things like, "I did really good on that test," or, "I'm good." Ugh! This is NOT the correct way to speak! In those sentences, the word "good" is being used to describe an action: how a person **did**, or how a person **is**. Therefore, the adverb "well" should be used. "I did really **well** on that test." "I'm **well**."
>
> The correct use of "well" and "good" can make or break a person's impression of your grammar – make sure to always speak correctly!

Study Tips for Improving Vocabulary and Grammar

1. Visit the Online Writing Lab website, which is sponsored by Purdue University, at http://owl.english.purdue.edu. This site provides you with an excellent overview of syntax, writing style, and strategy. It also has helpful and lengthy review sections that include multiple-choice "Test Your Knowledge" quizzes, which provide immediate answers to the questions.

2. It's beneficial to read the entire passage first to determine its intended meaning BEFORE you attempt to answer any questions. Doing so provides you with key insight into a passage's syntax (especially verb tense, subject-verb agreement, modifier placement, writing style, and punctuation).

3. When you answer a question, use the "Process-of-Elimination Method" to determine the best answer. Try each of the four answers and determine which one BEST fits with the meaning of the paragraph. Find the BEST answer. Chances are that the BEST answer is the CORRECT answer.

Practice Sentence Improvement

To give you a better idea of what you can expect from this section of the test, here are a few sample sentence improvement questions.

Paragraph A
Of the two types of eclipses, the most common is the lunar eclipse, which occurs when a full moon passes through Earth's shadow. (1) The disc-shaped moon slowly disappears completely or turns a coppery red color. (2) Solar and lunar eclipses both occur from time to time. (3)

Paragraph B
During a solar eclipse, the moon passes between the Earth and Sun. (4) As the moon moves into alignment, it blocks the light from the Sun creating an eerie darkness. (5) When the moon is perfectly in position, the Sun's light is visible as a ring, or corona, around the dark disc of the moon. (6) A lunar eclipse can be viewed from anywhere on the nighttime half of Earth, a solar eclipse can only be viewed from a zone that is only about 200 miles wide and covers about one-half of a percent of Earth's total area. (7)

1. Sentence 1: "Of the two types of eclipses, the most common is the lunar eclipse, which occurs when a full moon passes through Earth's shadow." What correction should be made to this sentence?
    a) Change "most" to "more."
    b) Change "occurs" to "occur."
    c) Change "which" to "that."
    d) Change "Earth's" to "Earths'."
    e) No correction is necessary.

2. Sentence 2: "The disc-shaped moon slowly disappears completely or turns a coppery red color." If you rewrote sentence 2, beginning with "<u>The disc-shaped moon slowly turns a coppery red color</u>," the next word should be:
    a) And.
    b) But.
    c) When.
    d) Because.
    e) Or.

3. Which revision would improve the effectiveness of paragraph A?
    a) Remove sentence 1.
    b) Move sentence 2 to the beginning of the paragraph.
    c) Remove sentence 2.
    d) Move sentence 3 to the beginning of the paragraph.
    e) No revision is necessary.

4. Sentence 7: "A lunar eclipse can be viewed from anywhere on the nighttime half of <u>Earth, a solar eclipse</u> can only be viewed from a zone that is only about 200 miles wide and covers about one-half of a percent of Earth's total area." Which of the following is the best way to write the underlined portion of this sentence? If the original is the best way, choose option **a)**.

    a) "Earth, a solar eclipse"
    b) "Earth a solar eclipse"
    c) "Earth; a solar eclipse"
    d) "Earth, because a solar eclipse"
    e) "Earth, when a solar eclipse"

Answers:

1. a)
Use the comparative "more" when comparing only two things. Here, you comparing two types of eclipses, so "more" is correct. The other changes introduce errors.

2. e)
The clauses are joined by the conjunction "or" in the original sentence. Maintaining this conjunction maintains the original relationship between ideas.

3. d)
As sentence 3 would serve as a good topic sentence, as well as an effective lead into sentence 1, the paragraph could be improved by moving sentence 3 to the beginning.

4. c)
The two related sentences should be separated by a semicolon. The other answers introduce incorrect punctuation or an inaccurate relationship between the sentences.

PART TWO: THE ESSAY SECTION

During this portion of the test, you will be provided a prompt, for which you will need to write a 250 word essay in 45 minutes or less. You will need to write an essay that is focused, organized, well-developed and supported, free of errors (usage, spelling, mechanics), and that has proper sentence structure.

This may sound like a tall order, but you can do it! The only way to prepare for this section is to practice writing timed essays. Your essay will be read by two different people, and given two separate scores from 1 to 4 (4 being the highest); these two scores are then averaged together for your final essay score. Be warned: If your final essay score is less than a 2, then you will need to retake both parts of the Language Arts – Writing test.

An Effective Essay Demonstrates:

1. Insightful and effective development of a point-of-view on the issue.

2. Critical thinking skills. For example: Two oppositions are given; instead of siding with one, you provide examples in which both would be appropriate.

3. Organization. It is clearly focused and displays a smooth progression of ideas.

4. Supportive information. If a statement is made, it is followed by examples, reasons, or other supporting evidence.

5. Skillful use of varied, accurate, and apt vocabulary.

6. Sentence variety. (Not every sentence follows a "subject-verb" pattern. Mix it up!)

7. Proper grammar and spelling.

Essay Examples and Evaluations

Here we will provide a sample TASC essay prompt, followed by four short sample responses. The four sample responses each display different qualities of work; an explanation will follow each sample, explaining what score it would have earned and why.

Prompt:

Research tells us that what children learn in their earliest years is very important to their future success in school. Because of this, public schools all over the country are starting to offer Pre-Kindergarten classes.

What are the benefits of starting school early? What are some of the problems you see in sending four-year-olds to school?

Write a composition in which you weigh the pros and cons of public school education for Pre-Kindergartners. Give reasons and specific examples to support your opinion. There is no specific word limit for your composition, but it should be long enough to give a clear and complete presentation of your ideas.

Sample Score 4 Essay

Today, more and more four-year-olds are joining their big brothers and sisters on the school bus and going to Pre-Kindergarten. Although the benefits of starting school early are clear, it is also clear that Pre-K is not for every child.

The students who are successful in Pre-K are ahead when they start kindergarten. Pre-K teaches them to play well with others. Even though it does not teach skills like reading and writing, it does help to prepare students for "real" school. Pre-K students sing songs, dance, paint and draw, climb and run. They learn to share and to follow directions. They tell stories and answer questions, and as they do, they add new words to their vocabularies. Pre-K can also give students experiences they might not get at home. They might take trips to the zoo or the farm, have visits from musicians or scientists, and so on. These experiences help the students better understand the world.

There are, however, some real differences among children of this age. Some four-year-olds are just not ready for the structure of school life. Some have a hard time leaving home, even for only three or four hours a day. Other children may already be getting a great preschool education at home or in daycare.

While you weigh the advantages and disadvantages of Pre-K, it is safe to say that each child is different. For some children, it is a wonderful introduction to the world of school. But others may not or should not be forced to attend Pre-K.

Evaluation of Sample Score 4 Essay

This paper is clearly organized and has stated a definite point of view. The paper opens with an introduction and closes with a conclusion. The introduction and conclusion combine an expression of the writer's opinion. Connections to the writer's opinion are made throughout the paper.

Sample Score 3 Essay

Just like everything in life, there are pros and cons to early childhood education. Pre-K classes work for many children, but they aren't for everyone. The plusses of Pre-K are obvious. Pre-K children learn many skills that will help them in kindergarten and later on. Probably the most important thing they learn is how to follow directions. This is a skill they will need at all stages of their life.

Other plusses include simple tasks like cutting, coloring in the lines, and learning capital letters. Many children don't get these skills at home. They need Pre-K to prepare them for kindergarten.

The minuses of Pre-K are not as obvious, but they are real. Children at this young age need the comfort of home. They need to spend time with parents, not strangers. They need that security. If parents are able to, they can give children the background they need to do well in school.

Other minuses include the fact that a lot of four year-old children can't handle school. They don't have the maturaty to sit still, pay attention, or share with others. Given another year, they may mature enough to do just fine in school. Sometimes it's better just to wait.

So there are definitely good things about Pre-K programs in our public schools, and I would definitely want to see one in our local schools. However, I think parents should decide whether their children are ready for a Pre-K education or not.

Evaluation of Sample Score 3 Essay

This paper has an identifiable organization plan, with pros and cons listed in order. The development is easy to understand, if not somewhat simplistic. The language of the paper is uneven, with some vague turns of phrase: "Just like everything in life," "definitely some good things." The word "maturity" is also misspelled. However, the essay is clear and controlled, and generally follows written conventions. If the writer had included more developed and explicit examples and used more varied words, this paper might have earned a higher score.

Sample Score 2 Essay

Is early childhood education a good idea? It depends on the child you're talking about. Some children probally need more education in the early years and need something to do to keep out of trouble. Like if there isnt any good nursry school or day care around it could be very good to have Pre-Kindergarten at the school so those children could have a good start on life. A lot of skills could be learned in Pre-Kindergarten, for example they could learn to write their name, cut paper, do art, etc.

Of course theres some kids who wouldnt do well, acting out and so on, so they might do better staying home than going to Pre-Kindergarten, because they just arent ready for school, and maybe wouldn't even be ready for kindergarten the next year either. Some kids just act younger than others or are too baby-ish for school.

So I would suport Pre-Kindergarten in our schools, it seems like a good idea to have someplace for those kids to go. Even if some kids wouldnt do well I think enough kids would do well, and it would make a diference in their grades as they got older. All those skills that they learned would help them in the future. If we did have Pre-Kindergarten it would help their working parents too, knowing their kids were someplace safe and learning importent things for life.

Evaluation of Sample Score 2 Essay

Although the writer of this paper has some good points to make, a lack of language skills, considerable misspellings, and a certain disconnectedness of thought keep the paper from scoring high. The paper begins with a vague introduction of the topic and ends with a paragraph that expresses the author's opinion, but the rest of the paper is disorganized. The reasons given do not always have examples to support them, and the examples that are given are weak.

Sample Score 1 to 2 Essay

What are benefits? What are some of problems with sending four-year-olds to school? Well, for one problem, its hard to see how little kids would do with all those big kids around at the school. They might get bullyed or lern bad habits, so I wouldnt want my four year old around those big kids on the bus and so on. Its hard to see how that could be good for a four year old. In our area we do have Pre-Kindergarten at our school but you dont have to go there a lot of kids in the program, I think about 50 or more, you see them a lot on the play ground mostly all you see them do is play around so its hard to see how that could be too usefull. They could play around at home just as easy. A reason for not doing Pre-Kindergarten is then what do you learn in Kindergarten. Why go do the same thing two years when you could just do one year when your a little bit bigger (older). I wonder do the people who want Pre-Kindergarten just want there kids out of the house or a baby sitter for there kids. Its hard to see why do we have to pay for that. I dont even know if Kindergarten is so usefull anyway, not like first grade where you actually learn something. So I would say theres lots of problems with Pre-Kindergarten.

Evaluation of Sample Score 1 to 2 Essay

This paper barely responds to the prompt. It gives reasons not to support Pre-K instruction, but it does not present any benefits of starting school early. The writer repeats certain phrases ("It's hard to see") to no real effect, and the faulty spelling, grammar, and punctuation significantly impede understanding. Several sentences wander off the topic entirely ("there a lot of kids in the program, I think about 50 or more, you see them a lot on the playground.", "I dont even know if Kindergarten is so usefull anyway, not like first grade where you actually learn something."). Instead of opening with an introduction, the writer simply lifts phrases from the prompt. The conclusion states the writer's opinion, but the reasons behind it are illogical and vague. Rather than organizing the essay in paragraph form, the writer has written a single, run-on paragraph. The lack of organization, weak language skills, and failure to address the prompt earn this essay a 2.

Test Your Knowledge: Language Arts – The Writing Section: Part One – The Multiple-Choice Section

Questions 1 – 5 are based on the following original passage. Sentences are numbered at the end for easy reference within the questions.

Examining the impact my lifestyle has on the earth's resources is, I believe, a fascinating and valuable thing to do (1). According to the Earth Day Network ecological footprint calculator, it would take four planet earths to sustain the human population if everyone used as many resources as I do (2). My "ecological footprint," or the amount of productive area of the earth that is required to produce the resources I consume, is therefore larger than the footprints of most of the population (3). It is hard to balance the luxuries and opportunities I have available to me with doing what I know to be better from an ecological standpoint (4).

It is fairly easy for me to recycle, so I do it, but it would be much harder to forgo the opportunity to travel by plane or eat my favorite fruits that have been flown to the supermarket from a different country (5). Although I get ecological points for my recycling habits, my use of public transportation, and living in an apartment complex rather than a free-standing residence, <u>my footprint expands when it is taken into account my not-entirely-local diet</u>, my occasional use of a car, my three magazine subscriptions, and my history of flying more than ten hours a year (6). I feel that realizing just how unfair my share of the earth's resources have been should help me to change at least some of my bad habits (7).

1. Which of the following is the best version of sentence 1?
   a) It is fascinating and valuable to examine the impact that my lifestyle has on the earth's resources.
   b) Examining the impact my lifestyle has on the earth's resources is a fascinating and valuable thing to do.
   c) To examine the impact my lifestyle has on the earth's resources is fascinating and is also valuable.
   d) The impact of my lifestyle on the earth's resources is fascinating and valuable to examine.
   e) Examining the impact my lifestyle has on the earth's resources is, I believe, a fascinating and valuable thing to do.

2. Sentence 4 would best fit if it were moved where in this composition?
   a) At the beginning of paragraph 2.
   b) After sentence 5.
   c) After sentence 6.
   d) At the end of paragraph 2.
   e) Sentence 4 is best left where it is.

3. Which two sentences would be improved by switching positions?
   a) 1 and 2.
   b) 3 and 4.
   c) 5 and 6.
   d) 6 and 7.
   e) 2 and 7.

4. How could sentences 2 and 3 best be combined?
   a) According to the Earth Day Network ecological footprint calculator, it would take four planet earths to sustain the human population if everyone used as many resources as I do because I have a very large "ecological footprint," which is the amount of productive area of the earth that is required to produce the resources I consume.
   b) According to the Earth Day Network ecological footprint calculator, which calculates the amount of productive area of the earth that is required to produce the resources one consumes, it would take four planet earths to sustain the human population if everyone had a footprint as large as mine.
   c) According to the Earth Day Network ecological footprint calculator, it would take four planet earths to sustain the human population if everyone used as many resources as I do; my "ecological footprint," or the amount of productive area of the earth that is required to produce the resources I consume, is therefore larger than the footprints of most of the population.
   d) According to the Earth Day Network ecological footprint calculator, which measures the amount of productive area of the earth that is required to produce the resources a person consumes, my footprint is larger than that of most; it would take four planet earths to sustain the human population if everyone consumed as much as I do.
   e) According to the Earth Day Network ecological footprint calculator, my "ecological footprint," or the amount of productive area of the earth that is required to produce the resources I consume, would require four planet earths if it were to be the footprint of the human population; it is therefore larger than the footprints of most of the population.

5. Which of the following should replace the underlined portion of sentence 6?
   a) "my footprint expands when taken into account my not-entirely-local diet"
   b) "my footprint expands when taken into account are my not-entirely-local diet"
   c) "my footprint expands when we take into account my not-entirely-local diet"
   d) "my footprint expands when one takes into account my not-entirely-local diet"
   e) "my footprint expands when it is taken into account my not-entirely-local diet"

6. Which revision would most improve sentence 7?
   a) Eliminate the phrase "I feel that."
   b) Change "should help me" to "will help me."
   c) Add the phrase "In conclusion," to the beginning.
   d) Change "have been" to "has been."
   e) Eliminate the phrase "at least some of."

Questions 7 – 12 are based on the short passage below, which is excerpted from Thomas Huxley's preface to his Collected Essays: Volume V (public domain) and modified slightly. Sentences are numbered at the end for easy reference within the questions.

I had set out on a journey, with no other purpose than that of exploring a certain province of natural knowledge, I strayed no hair's breadth from the course which it was my right and my duty to pursue; and yet I found that, whatever route I took, before long, I came to a tall and formidable-looking fence (1). Confident I might be in the existence of an ancient and indefeasible right of way, before me stood the thorny barrier with its comminatory notice-board—"No Thoroughfare. By order" (2). There seemed no way over; nor did the prospect of creeping round, as I saw some do, attracts me (3). True there was no longer any cause to fear the spring guns and man-traps set by former lords of the manor; but one is apt to get very dirty going on all-fours (4). The only alternatives were either to give up my journey—which I was not minded to do—or to break the fence down and go through it (5). I swiftly ruled out crawling under as an option (6). I also ruled out turning back (7).

7. How could sentence 1 best be changed?
    a) The comma after journey should be removed.
    b) The comma after knowledge should be changed to a semicolon.
    c) "and yet" should be eliminated.
    d) Change "I had set out" to "I set out."
    e) No change.

8. Sentence 6 should be placed where in the passage?
    a) After sentence 1.
    b) After sentence 2.
    c) After sentence 3.
    d) After sentence 4.
    e) Left after sentence 5.

9. Which edit should be made in sentence 3?
    a) "nor" should be changed to "or."
    b) "seemed" should be changed to "seems."
    c) "me" should be changed to "I."
    d) "attracts" should be changed to "attract."
    e) No edit should be made.

10. How could sentences 6 and 7 best be combined?
    a) Swiftly, I ruled out crawling under as an option and also turning back.
    b) Ruling out two options swiftly: crawling under and turning back.
    c) I swiftly ruled out the options of crawling under or turning back.
    d) I ruled out crawling under as an option and I swiftly also ruled out turning back.
    e) I swiftly ruled out crawling under as an option and also turning back.

11. Which word could be inserted at the beginning of sentence 2 before "confident" to best clarify the meaning?

    a) Even.
    b) However.
    c) Hardly.
    d) Finally.
    e) Especially.

12. Which of the following is the best way to split sentence 1 into two separate sentences?

    a) I had set out on a journey, with no other purpose than that of exploring a certain province of natural knowledge. I strayed no hair's breadth from the course which it was my right and my duty to pursue; and yet I found that, whatever route I took, before long, I came to a tall and formidable-looking fence.

    b) I had set out on a journey, with no other purpose than that of exploring a certain province of natural knowledge, I strayed no hair's breadth from the course which it was my right and my duty to pursue. Yet I found that, whatever route I took, before long, I came to a tall and formidable-looking fence.

    c) I had set out on a journey, with no other purpose than that of exploring a certain province of natural knowledge, I strayed no hair's breadth from the course which it was my right and my duty to pursue; and yet I found that, whatever route I took, before long. I came to a tall and formidable-looking fence.

    d) I had set out on a journey. With no other purpose than that of exploring a certain province of natural knowledge, I strayed no hair's breadth from the course which it was my right and my duty to pursue; and yet I found that, whatever route I took, before long, I came to a tall and formidable-looking fence.

    e) I had set out on a journey, with no other purpose than that of exploring a certain province of natural knowledge, I strayed no hair's breadth from the course which it was my right and my duty to pursue; and yet. I found that, whatever route I took, before long, I came to a tall and formidable-looking fence.

Questions 13 – 27 are based on the short passage below:

Sandra Cisneros, perhaps the best known Latina author in the United States, writes poems and stories whose titles alone – "Barbie-Q," "My Lucy Friend Who Smells Like Corn," "Woman Hollering Creek" – engage potential readers' curiosity. (1) Ironically, this renowned writer, whose books are printed on recycled paper, did not do wellin school. (2) When she lectures at schools and public libraries, Cisneros presents the evidence. (3) An elementary school report card containing Cs, Ds and a solitary B (for conduct). (4) Cisneros has a theory to explain her low grades: teachers had low expectations for Latina and Latino students from Chicago's South Side. (5) Despite the obstacles that she faced in school, Cisneros completed not only high school but also college. (6) Her persistence paid off in her twenties, when Cisneros was admitted <u>prestigious</u> to the Writers' Workshop at the University of Iowa. (7)

Cisneros <u>soon</u> observed that most of her classmates at the university seemed to have a common set of memories, based on middle-class childhoods, from which to draw in their writing. (8) Cisneros felt <u>decided</u> out of place. _____("9A")_____. (9) She decided to speak from her own experience. (10) Her voice, which by being one of a Latina living outside of the mainstream, found a large and attentive audience in 1984 with the publication of her first short story collection, The House on Mango Street. (11) <u>Today</u> the book is read by middle school, high school, and college students across the United States. (12) Cisneros uses her influence as a successful writer to help other Latina and Latino writers get their works published. (13) But <u>having made the argument that</u>, in order for large numbers of young Latinos to achieve literary success, the educational system itself must change. (14) Cisneros <u>hints</u> that she succeeded in spite of the educational system. "I'm the exception," she insists, "not the rule." (15)

13. What change should be made to sentence 1?
   a) No Change.
   b) "author and writer."
   c) "author and novelist."
   d) "wordsmith and author."

14. What change should be made towards the end of sentence 1?
   a) No Change.
   b) "potential, reader's."
   c) "potential, readers."
   d) "potential readers."

15. What change should be made to sentence 2?
   a) No Change.
   b) "writer, who is recognized by her orange and black eyeglasses"
   c) "writer, who likes to write at night,"
   d) "writer"

16. What change should be made to sentence 3?
   a) No Change.
   b) "evidence: an"
   c) "evidence; an"
   d) "evidence an"

17. The best placement for the underlined portion in sentence 7 would be:
   a) Where it is now.
   b) Before the word admitted.
   c) Before the word "Writers'."
   d) Before the word "Workshop."

18. Which word would best replace the underlined portion in sentence 8?
   a) No Change.
   b) "furthermore"
   c) "nevertheless"
   d) "therefore"

19. Which of the following is the best beginning of sentence 9?
  a) No Change.
  b) "Cisneros herself,"
  c) "Cisneros, herself"
  d) "Cisneros,"

20. Which of the following is should replace the underlined word in sentence 9?
  a) No Change.
  b) "deciding"
  c) "decidedly"
  d) "decidedly and"

21. Which of the following true statements, if added at _____("9A")_____ , would best serve as a transition between the challenges Cisneros faced as an aspiring writer and her success in meeting those challenges?
  a) "She did not know what to do."
  b) "Then she had a break through."
  c) "At that point she almost went home to Chicago."
  d) "She wondered whether she was in the right field."

22. Which of the following changes should be made to sentence 11?
  a) No Change.
  b) "voice – that of a Latina living outside the mainstream –"
  c) "voice, being one of a Latina living outside the mainstream, it"
  d) "voice – in which it was a Latina living outside the mainstream –"

23. Which of the following changes should be made to sentence 11?
  a) No Change.
  b) "1984, With"
  c) "1984; with"
  d) "1984, with,"

24. Which of the following is the best change to the underlined word at the beginning of sentence 12?
  a) No Change.
  b) "In the future,"
  c) "Meanwhile,"
  d) "At the same time,"

25. Which of the following is the best replacement for the underlined portion in sentence 14?
  a) No Change.
  b) "she argues that,"
  c) "arguing that,"
  d) "she argues that, when"

26. Which choice best shows that Cisneros is emphatic about expressing the belief stated in the underlined portion of sentence 15?
   a) No Change.
   b) "Says."
   c) "Supposes."
   d) "Asserts."

27. The writer is considering deleting the last sentence. If the writer decided to delete this sentence, the paragraph would primarily lose a statement that:
   a) Enhances the subject and setting.
   b) Provides support for a point previously made.
   c) Humorously digresses from the main topic of the paragraph.
   d) Contradicts Cisneros's claim made earlier in the essay.

Questions 28-40 are based on the short passage below:

Traveling on commercial airlines has changed substantially <u>over years</u>. (1) When commercial air travel first became available, it was so expensive that usually only businessmen could afford <u>to do so</u>. (2) Airplane efficiency, the relative cost of fossil fuels, <u>and using economies</u> of scale have all contributed to make travel by air more affordable and common. (3) These days, there are nearly 30,000 commercial air flights in the world each day! (4)

Depending on the size of the airport you are departing from, you should arrive 90 minutes to two and a half hours before your plane leaves. (5) Things like checking your luggage and flying internationally can make the process of getting to your gate take longer. (6) If you fly out of a very busy airport, like <u>LaGuardia, in</u> New York City, on a very busy travel day, like the day before Thanksgiving, you can easily miss your flight if you don't arrive early enough. (7)

Security processes for passengers have also changed. (8) In the 1960s, there was <u>hardly any</u> security: you could just buy your ticket and walk on to the plane the day of the flight without even needing to show identification. (9) In the 1970s, American commercial airlines started installing sky marshals on many <u>flights, an</u> undercover law enforcement officers who would protect the passengers from a potential hijacking. (10)

Also in the early 1970s, the federal government began to require that airlines screen passengers and their luggage for things like weapons and bombs. (11) After the 2001 terrorist attacks in the United States, these requirements were <u>stringently enforced</u>. (12) Family members can no longer meet someone at the <u>gate; only ticketed passengers are allowed into the gate area</u>. (13) The definition of <u>weapons are</u> not allowed is expanded every time there is a new incident for example liquids are now restricted on planes after an attempted planned attack using gel explosives in 2006. (14)

Despite the hassles of traveling by air, it is still a boon to modern <u>life. (15) Still, some </u>businesses are moving away from sending employees on airplane trips, <u>as</u> face-to-face video conferencing technologies improve. (16) A trip which might take ten hours by car <u>can take only</u> two hours by plane. (17) However, the ability to travel quickly by air <u>will always be valued, by citizens</u> of our modern society. (18)

28. Which of the following is the best change to the underlined portion of sentence 1?
 a) No Change.
 b) "over the years"
 c) "over time"
 d) Delete.

29. Which of the following is the best change to the underlined portion of sentence 2?
 a) No Change.
 b) "to do it"
 c) "to fly"
 d) "do so"

30. Which of the following is the best change to the underlined portion of sentence 3?
 a) No Change.
 b) "using economies"
 c) "and the use of economies"
 d) "and economies"

31. Which of the following is the best change to the underlined portion of sentence 7?
 a) No Change.
 b) "La Guardia in"
 c) "La Guardia; in"
 d) "La Guardia,"

32. Which of the following is the best change to the underlined portion of sentence 9?
 a) No Change.
 b) "hardly"
 c) "no"
 d) "barely"

33. Which of the following is the best change to the underlined portion of sentence 10?
 a) No Change.
 b) "flights; an"
 c) "flights. Marshals are"
 d) "flights, marshals are"

34. Which of the following is the best change to the underlined portion of sentence 12?
 a) No Change.
 b) "stiffly upheld"
 c) "enforced with more stringency"
 d) "more stringently enforced"

35. If the underlined portion in sentence 13 were deleted, the passage would lose:
 a) No Change.
 b) An explanation of the screening process.
 c) Ambiguity over why family members are no longer allowed at the gate.
 d) A further specific example of how regulations have changed over time.

36. Which of the following is the best change to the underlined portion in sentence 14?
 a) No Change.
 b) "weapon is"
 c) "weapons"
 d) "weapons which are"

37. Which of the following is the proper transition between sentences 15 & 16?
 a) No Change.
 b) "life. Some"
 c) "life even though some"
 d) "life, still some"

38. Which of the following is the best replacement for the underlined word in sentence 16?
 a) No Change.
 b) "because"
 c) "while"
 d) "since"

39. Which of the following is the best change to the underlined portion in sentence 17?
 a) No Change.
 b) "may only take"
 c) "takes only"
 d) "will only take"

40. Which of the following is the best change to the underlined portion in sentence 18?
 a) No Change.
 b) "citizens will always value"
 c) "will always, be valued by citizens"
 d) "will always be valued by citizens"

Test Your Knowledge: Language Arts – The Writing Section: Part One – The Multiple-Choice Section – Answers

1. a).

2. c).

3. c).

4. d).

5. d).

6. d).

7. b).

8. d).

9. d).

10. c).

11. b).

12. a).

13. a).

14. a).

15. d).

16. b).

17. c).

18. a).

19. a).

20. c).

21. b).

22. b).

23. a).

24. a).

25. b).

26. d).

27. b).

28. b).

29. c).

30. c).

31. b).

32. a).

33. c).

34. d).

35. d).

36. d).

37. c).

38. a).

39. b).

40. d).

Test Your Knowledge: Language Arts – The Writing Section:
Part Two – The Essay Section

Prompt One

Provided below is an excerpt and a question. Use the excerpt to prompt your thinking, and then plan and write an essay in 45 minutes by answering the question from your perspective. Be sure to provide evidence.

- *General George S. Patton Jr. is quoted as having said, "No good decision was ever made in a swivel chair."*

Is it necessary to be directly in a situation in order to best understand what must be done?

Prompt Two

Provided below is an excerpt and a question. Use the excerpt to prompt your thinking, and then plan and write an essay in 45 minutes by answering the question from your perspective. Be sure to provide evidence.

- *In The Dispossessed, published in 1974, groundbreaking science fiction author Ursula K. LeGuin wrote, "You can't crush ideas by suppressing them. You can only crush them by ignoring them."*

Is it possible to get rid of an idea?

Prompt Three

Provided below is an excerpt and a question. Use the excerpt to prompt your thinking, and then plan and write an essay in 45 minutes by answering the question from your perspective. Be sure to provide evidence.

- *"The paradox of education is precisely this -- that as one begins to become conscious one begins to examine the society in which he is being educated." James Baldwin (1924-1987), American novelist, poet, and social critic*

Does a successful education require the examination of one's own society?

The following pages hold sample scored essays for topics one, two, and three. These are just examples – there are many ways that essays can be scored high or low. Look for: reasoning, examples, word usage, coherency, and detail. There are no "right" answers on the essay; the most important factor is that the argument be well-developed.

Essays for Prompt One

Is it necessary to be directly in a situation to best understand what must be done?

Score of 3 – 4:

General George Patton was speaking of war when he noted that "no good decision was ever made in a swivel chair;" however, that observation applies to situations beyond battle. While a big-picture perspective is useful in analyzing situations and deciding how to act, an on-the-ground outlook is essential. In matters of politics, and technology, to name two, the best-laid plans usually have to be changed to respond to changing circumstances.

One example which illustrates the necessity of on-the-ground action is the famous space flight of Apollo 13. Before launch, all plans were worked out to get the manned mission to the moon and back. However, due to a fluke set of circumstances – an oxygen tank explosion and the resulting technical problems – the plans had to change. The successful return of Apollo 13 and the survival of its crew would not have been possible without the quick thinking of the men on board. They first noticed the incident, well before the technical crew in Houston would have detected it from Earth. While the work of the technical crew was of course key as well, without the astronauts on board the ship to implement an emergency plan, the mission would surely have been lost.

Just as there are often unforeseen circumstances when implementing technology, politics can also be unpredictable. For example, the Cuban Missile Crisis in 1962 required immediate, on-the-ground decision making by the leaders of the United States. Prior to the Cold War standoff, President Kennedy and his advisors had already decided their hardline position against Soviet weapons expansion in the Western hemisphere. The Monroe Doctrine, status quo since the 1920s, held that European countries should not practice their influence in the Americas. The Soviet Union tested this line by establishing intermediate-range missiles on the island of Cuba. President Kennedy could not simply hold to the established wisdom, because the true limits had never been tested. Instead, to stave off the threat of attack, he was forced to act immediately as events unfolded to preserve the safety of American lives. The crisis unfolded minute-by-minute, with formerly confident advisors unsure of the smartest step. Eventually, after thirteen tense days, the leaders were able to reach a peaceful conclusion.

What these events of the 1960s illustrate is that the best laid plans are often rendered useless by an unfolding situation. For crises to be resolved, whether they be in war, technology, or politics; leaders must have level heads in the moment with up-to-date information. Therefore, plans established in advance by those in swivel chairs with level heads are not always the best plans to follow. History has shown us that we must be able to think on our feet as unforeseen situations unfold.

Score of 2 – 3:

It is often necessary to be directly on the ground as a situation unfolds to know what is best do to. This is because situations can be unpredictable and what you previously thought was the best course of action, is not always so. This can be seen in the unfolding events of the 1962 Cuban Missile Crisis.

The Cuban Missile Crisis happened in 1962, during the presidency of John F. Kennedy, when Nikita Khrushchev, president of the Soviet Union, developed an intermediate-range missile base on the island of Cuba, within range of the United States. Since the Monroe Doctrine in the 1920s, the United States leaders have declared that they would not tolerate this kind of aggression. However, the decisions that had been made by leaders in the past, removed from the situation, were no longer relevant. It was necessary for President Kennedy to make decisions as events unfolded.

As the Cuban Missile Crisis shows us, at turning points in history decisions have to be made as events unfold by those who are in the middle of a situation. Otherwise, we would all be acting according to what those in the past and those removed from the challenge thought was best. Following the Monroe Doctrine could have resulted in unnecessary violence.

Score of 2 or Less:

It is necessary to make decisions while in the middle of a situation, not above the situation, because there is always information that is only known to people in the middle of the situation. For example, in a war, the strategists in Washington might have an overall aim in the war, but they would be unable to know what it best to do on the ground. Situations like running out of ammunition or the enemy having an unexpected backup could change the decisions that need to be made. This was especially true before cell phones and other digital technologies made communication easier.

Essays for Prompt Two

Is it possible to get rid of an idea?

Score of 3 – 4:

The suppression of ideas has been attempted over and over throughout history by different oppressive regimes. This theme has been explored as well in literature, through such dystopian works as 1984 and Fahrenheit 451. But these histories and stories always play out the same way: eventually, the repressed idea bubbles to the surface and triumphs. Ursula K. LeGuin acknowledged this by saying that ideas can be crushed not by suppression, but by omission.

In Aldous Huxley's novel Brave New World, the world government maintains order not by governing people strictly and policing their ideas, but by distracting them. Consumption is the highest value of the society. When an outsider to the society comes in and questions it, he is exiled – not to punish him, but to remove his influence from society. The government of the dystopia has learned that the best way to maintain control is to keep citizens unaware of other, outside ideas. This theme resonates with a modern audience more than other, more authoritarian tales of dystopia because in our society, we are less controlled than we are influenced and persuaded.

Repressing ideas through harsh authoritarian rule has proven time and again to be ultimately fruitless. For example, in Soviet Russia during the 1920s and 1930s, Josef Stalin attempted to purge his society of all religious belief. This was done through suppression: discriminatory laws were enacted, members of the clergy were executed, and the religious citizenry were terrified. While these measures drastically crippled religious institutions, they were ineffective at completely eliminating the idea of religion. Beliefs and traditions were passed down in communities clandestinely throughout the repressive rule of Stalin. After the fall of the Soviet Union, it became clear that religion had survived all along.

We see throughout literature and history that ignoring ideas and distracting people from them is generally more effective than to attempt to stamp an idea out through means of suppression. Authoritarian rule, in fact, can do the opposite: by dramatizing and calling attention to an idea in the name of condemning it, a regime might actually strengthen that idea.

Score of 2 – 3:

We have seen different governments try to crush out ideas throughout history. However, they are never actually successful in doing so. An idea can be ignored or suppressed, but it will never really go away. This is illustrated in the survival of religion in the Soviet Union.

In Soviet Russia during the 1920s and 1930s, Josef Stalin attempted to purge the society of all religious belief. This was done through suppression: discriminatory laws, execution of the clergy, and use of terror. While this harmed religious institutions, they were ineffective at crushing the idea of religion. Beliefs and traditions were passed down in communities secretly throughout the rule of Stalin. After the fall of the Soviet Union, it became clear that religion had survived all along.

The same kind of thing happened with apartheid law in South Africa. Even though there were laws against black Africans and white Africans using the same facilities, the idea caught fire, especially because of an international outcry against the law.

We see throughout history that suppressing ideas does not crush them. Authoritarian rule, in fact, can do the opposite: by calling attention to an idea in the name of condemning it, a regime might actually strengthen that idea.

Score of 2 or Less:

It is not possible to crush out an idea by ignoring it or by suppressing it. All throughout history, whenever anyone has tried to do this, they might be temporarily successful but the idea will always survive or come back. For example in the Soviet Union religion was suppressed. People were not allowed to practice their religion. But after the government fell, religion still existed – people had held on to their ideas during the time of suppression.

Essays for Prompt Three

Does a successful education require the examination of one's own society?

Score of 3 – 4:

James Baldwin noted that education is a paradox – as one becomes educated, one starts to question the educators. This is necessarily true, because an education is not just a mastery of facts and information but also acquiring the ability to think critically and forge new connections. Progress in society comes from people who understand the thought that came before and are then able to take it one step further. This theme plays out in social activism and in science, for example.

A society's understanding of human rights is constantly evolving. For this process to continue, each generation must question the mores taught by the previous generation. This process can be seen in America in the progression of women's rights, the rights of non-whites, religious rights, and the rights of the disabled. One hundred years ago, these groups had far less constitutional protection than they do today. It takes groups of educated people with a forward-thinking understanding to advocate and press for changes to be made. To take one example, women have gone from not having the right to vote in 1912 to, one hundred years later, women beginning to run for the highest political office. This happened because people like Elizabeth Cady Stanton, a suffragist in the 1850s, and Marsha Griffiths, the Representative in Congress in the 1970s who championed for the Equal Rights Amendment, were able to take the precepts of justice and equality taught to them and take them a step further by applying them to women's rights.

This pattern of taking knowledge a step further can also be seen in the fields of science and mathematics. Sir Isaac Newton, one of the inventors of calculus, is attributed with saying he "stood on the shoulders of giants." He took the concepts well established in mathematics – geometry and algebra – and used the tools in a new way to create calculus. To do this, he had to both already understand what was known in the field but also be able to look at it critically. Without people doing this, fields like science and math would never progress.

A society that is interested in advancing, in rights, science, and every other field, must educate its citizens not to only understand the knowledge of the past but also to criticize prior thought and look at things in a new way. This is what James Baldwin meant – a truly educated person will question everything, even his or her own society, in order to progress.

Score of 2 – 3:

James Baldwin noted that education is a paradox – as one becomes educated, one starts to question the educators. This is true because an education is not just a mastery of facts and information but also ability to think critically and forge new connections. Progress in society comes from people who understand the thought that came before and are then able to take it one step further. One example of this is in human and political rights.

A society's understanding of human rights is constantly evolving. For this process to continue, each generation must question the mores taught by the previous generation. This process can be seen in America in the progression of women's rights, the rights of non-whites, religious rights, and the rights of the disabled. One hundred years ago, these groups had far less constitutional protection than they do today. It takes groups of educated people with a forward-thinking understanding to press for changes to be made. To take one example, women have gone from not having the right to vote in 1912 to, one hundred years later, women beginning to run for the highest political office. This happened because people like Elizabeth Cady Stanton, a suffragist in the 1850s, and Marsha Griffiths, the Representative in Congress in the 1970s who championed for the Equal Rights Amendment, were able to take the precepts of justice and equality taught to them and take them a step further by applying them to women's rights.

A society that is interested in advancing, in rights every other field, must educate its citizens not to only understand the knowledge of the past but also to criticize prior thought and look at things in a new way. This is what James Baldwin meant – a truly educated person will question everything, even his or her own society, in order to progress.

Score of 2 or Less:

James Baldwin said that education is a paradox – as one becomes educated, one starts to question the educators. He is right about this, because being educated is not just about knowing the facts. It is also about critical thinking. Without thinking critically about one's own society, then people never make progress. This was necessary for things like civil rights, they could not just accept what was taught in the schools about the rights people should have. Probably the most important part of being educated is questioning the society you live in.

Chapter 3: Social Studies

The social studies section of the TASC consists of 47 multiple-choice questions. Generally, the ability to answer these questions relies heavily on reading comprehension. While you will need some specific previous knowledge, many of the questions can be answered by use of the information provided on the exam itself. Your skills of interpretation and inference are just as important on this section as they are in the Reading section. The questions will be presented in three forms: Prose only (Written Passages); Graphic or Visual only (cartoons, photos, maps, graphs, etc.); and Prose and Graphic combinations.

Within the 47 questions, four major content areas are tested:

History (U.S. specific – 12 questions; Global – 8 questions):
- Colonization through Westward Expansion.
- Civil War.
- Industrialization.
- Armed Conflict and Global Economic Depression.
- Postwar and Contemporary United States.
- Enduring Issues and Current Challenges.

Major Periods and Developments of World History:
- Early Civilizations and the Great Empires.
- World Religions.
- Feudalism through the Era of Expansion.
- Global Age.
- Revolutions.
- Armed Conflicts.
- 20th Century.

Economic Theory and Consumerism (approximately 10 questions):
- Economic Reasoning and Choice.
- Comparison of Modern Economic Systems.
- Production and Consumers.
- Financial Institutions.
- Government's Role in the Economy.
- Labor.
- Global Markets.

Geography – The World in Spatial Terms (approximately 7 questions):
- Places and Regions.
- Physical Systems.
- Human Systems.
- Environment and Society.
- Uses of Geography.

Test Your Knowledge: Social Studies

Questions 1 and 2 refer to the following passage:

The landmass area of the United States doubled in 1803 with the purchase of the Louisiana Territory from France, which included land from what is now Louisiana at the southern tip of the country all the way north to the Rocky Mountains in what is now parts of Montana and Minnesota. Thomas Jefferson, the president who brokered this deal, believed that the continued moral strength of the young nation depended on its citizens having ownership of farm land, to be able to work independently tilling the earth. However, the sale of this land was not without controversy: American politicians of the time debated whether it was constitutional or prudent to increase the size of the nation so rapidly, and it is questionable whether France had legally obtained the land from Spain and had the right to sell it at all.

1. Which of the following is true about the Louisiana Purchase?
   a) It involved a transaction between Spain and the United States.
   b) It was universally considered to be a good idea.
   c) It included territory that would become multiple states in the US.
   d) It tripled the landmass area of the United States.
   e) It guaranteed farm land for every American citizen.

2. Based on the information in the passage, which of the following might be a reason for an American politician of 1803 to oppose the Louisiana Purchase?
   a) The Constitution did not stipulate whether the nation could be increased in size.
   b) The price per acre of the land included was too high.
   c) Most of the soil in the regions of the Louisiana Territory is not good farmland.
   d) Giving citizens new areas to farm would strengthen the culture of the nation.
   e) France had legally obtained the territory from Spain.

Questions 3 and 4 refer to the following cartoon and information:

THE LAST FEW BUTTONS ARE ALWAYS THE HARDEST.

—Chapin in the St. Louis *Star.*

This cartoon was originally published in the St. Louis *Star* newspaper. Since 1807, only men had been legally allowed to vote in the United States. Suffragists, or activists for extending the right to vote to women, had been working for decades to overturn this. By the beginning of the 1900s, four states allowed women to vote at the state level. In 1918, the president of the United States, Woodrow Wilson, began to support women's suffrage. In June of 1919, the legislature passed the 19th Amendment, guaranteeing the right to vote to women. However, 36 state legislatures had to ratify, or approve, the amendment before it could be official. This took until August of 1920.

3. During which of the following months is this cartoon most likely to have been published?
    a) June 1901.
    b) August 1918.
    c) June 1919.
    d) March 1920.
    e) October 1920.

4. In the cartoon, the buttons represent what?
    a) Presidents who supported women's suffrage.
    b) The number of amendments that needed to be passed.
    c) States that are needed to ratify the 19th Amendment.
    d) Steps in the process of finalizing a bill.
    e) National legislators who voted for the passage of the 19th Amendment.

No country on the globe is so happily situated, or so internally capable of raising a fleet as America. Tar, timber, iron, and cordage are her natural produce. We need go abroad for nothing. Whereas the Dutch, who make large profits by hiring out their ships of war to the Spaniards and Portuguese, are obliged to import most of their materials they use. We ought to view the building a fleet as an article of commerce, it being the natural manufactory of this country. It is the best money we can lay out. A navy when finished is worth more than it cost. And is that nice point in national policy, in which commerce and protection are united. Let us build; if we want them not, we can sell; and by that means replace our paper currency with ready gold and silver…

In point of safety, ought we to be without a fleet? We are not the little people now, which we were sixty years ago; at that time we might have trusted our property in the streets, or fields rather; and slept securely without locks or bolts to our doors or windows. The case now is altered, and our methods of defense ought to improve with our increase of property. A common pirate, twelve months ago, might have come up the Delaware, and laid the city of Philadelphia under instant contribution, for what sum he pleased; and the same might have happened to other places. Nay, any daring fellow, in a brig of fourteen or sixteen guns might have robbed the whole continent, and carried off half a million of money. These are circumstances which demand our attention, and point out the necessity of naval protection.

Some, perhaps, will say, that after we have made it up with Britain, she will protect us. Can we be so unwise as to mean, that she shall keep a navy in our harbors for that purpose? Common sense will tell us, that the power which hath endeavored to subdue us, is of all others the most improper to defend us. Conquest may be affected under the pretense of friendship; and we after a long and brave resistance may be at last cheated into slavery. And if her ships are not to be admitted into our harbors, I would ask, how is she to protect us? A navy three or four thousand miles off can be of little use, and on sudden emergencies, none at all. Wherefore, if we must hereafter protect ourselves, why not do it for ourselves?

5. Thomas Paine indicates that what has changed over the past sixty years?
    a) The country now has enough tar, timber, and iron to build a fleet of ships.
    b) Pirates are now more common.
    c) The relationship between America and Britain is now much friendlier.
    d) The Dutch are no longer hiring out their ships of war.
    e) The American people now have much more property to protect.

6. All of the following are given as reasons why Americans should not rely on British military protection, EXCEPT:
    a) The British cannot be trusted to protect Americans.
    b) British ships may not be allowed into American harbors.
    c) The British navy may not be strong enough to defend America.
    d) The British navy may not always be close by enough to defend America.
    e) British ships could be used to undermine American independence from Britain.

7. The author would most likely agree with which of the following points?
   a) America should maintain independence from Britain.
   b) Policy-makers must choose between promoting protection or commerce.
   c) It is difficult to sell ships.
   d) It would be necessary to import ship-building materials to build the navy.
   e) The British navy could be an important supplement in protection.

Questions 8 and 9 use information from the graph below:

American Industrial Production Index, 1928 – 1939[4]

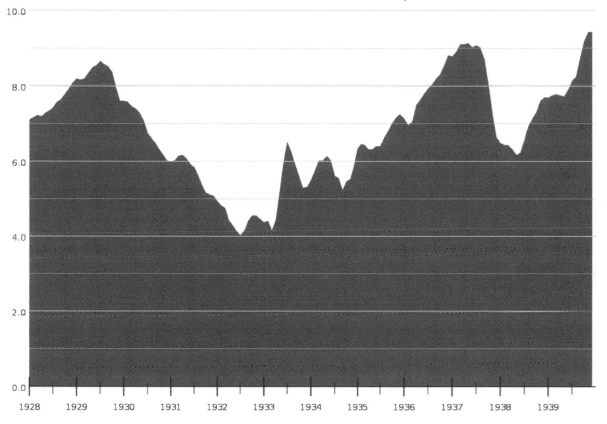

8. The longest period of the decline in American manufacturing and mining occurred when?
   a) 1928-1929.
   b) 1929-1932.
   c) 1933-1935.
   d) 1936-1938.
   e) 1938-1939.

---

[4] The Industrial Production Index measures the domestic output of manufactured and mined goods.
[5] Image Source: public domain image, data from the St. Louis Federal Reserve.

9. Which of the following events was likely to have happened, given the information in the graph?
   a) In 1929, demand for American-made goods increased abroad.
   b) In 1930, the downward trend in production was reversed due to foreign investment.
   c) In 1933, the government enacted measures to somewhat increase domestic production.
   d) In 1936, the global markets crashed again, leading to a dramatic dip in American production.
   e) In 1938, American production was at the pre-crash levels found in 1928.

Questions 10 through 12 use information found on the following map of Venezuela's roads:

[6] Map Source: The CIA World Factbook.

10. Venezuela can be driven into on a major road from which other countries?
    a) Brazil and Guyana.
    b) Columbia and Guyana.
    c) Brazil and Columbia.
    d) Brazil only.
    e) Columbia only.

11. Based on the information in the map, which of the following conclusions is likely?
    a) San Juan de Manapiare is a center of commerce.
    b) Railroads are heavily used for transporting products within Venezuela.
    c) Bogota is the political center of Venezuela.
    d) The Pan-American Highway is important to Venezuelan transportation.
    e) Bogota and Caracas are about 400 miles apart by highway.

12. Venezuela is a very highly urbanized country, with most of the population concentrated in the cities. Based on this information and the map, it is reasonable to assume that 95% of the population lives:
    a) In Caracas.
    b) In Ciudad Guyana.
    c) On the coast.
    d) North of Rio Orinoco.
    e) South of Rio Orinoco.

Below is the example of the 1099 tax form given by the Internal Revenue Service, the bureau of the United States government responsible for collecting taxes. Questions 13 and 14 refer to this form.

The completed Form 1099-MISC illustrates the following example. Z Builders is a contractor that subcontracts drywall work to Ronald Green, a sole proprietor who does business as Y Drywall. During the year, Z Builders pays Mr. Green $5,500. Z Builders must file Form 1099-MISC because they paid Mr. Green $600 or more in the course of their trade or business, and Mr. Green is not a corporation.

9595		☐ VOID	☐ CORRECTED		
PAYER'S name, street address, city or town, province or state, country, ZIP or foreign postal code, and telephone no. Z Builders 123 Maple Avenue Oaktown, AL 00000 555-555-1212		**1 Rents** $ **2 Royalties** $	OMB No. 1545-0115 20**13** Form **1099-MISC**	**Miscellaneous Income**	
		3 Other income $	**4 Federal income tax withheld** $	**Copy A** For **Internal Revenue Service Center**	
PAYER'S federal identification number	RECIPIENT'S identification number	**5 Fishing boat proceeds** $	**6 Medical and health care payments** $		
10-9999999	123-00-6789			File with Form 1096.	
RECIPIENT'S name Ronald Green dba/ Y Drywall		**7 Nonemployee compensation** $ 5500.00	**8 Substitute payments in lieu of dividends or interest** $	For Privacy Act and Paperwork Reduction Act Notice, see the **2013 General Instructions for Certain Information Returns.**	
Street address (including apt. no.) 456 Flower Lane		**9 Payer made direct sales of $5,000 or more of consumer products to a buyer (recipient) for resale ▶** ☐	**10 Crop insurance proceeds** $		
City or town, province or state, country, and ZIP or foreign postal code Oaktown, AL 00000		**11 Foreign tax paid** $	**12 Foreign country or U.S. possession**		
Account number (see instructions)	2nd TIN not. ☐	**13 Excess golden parachute payments** $	**14 Gross proceeds paid to an attorney** $		
15a Section 409A deferrals $	**15b Section 409A income** $	**16 State tax withheld** $	**17 State/Payer's state no.**	**18 State income** $ $	

Form **1099-MISC**   Cat. No. 14425J   www.irs.gov/form1099misc   Department of the Treasury - Internal Revenue Service

Do Not Cut or Separate Forms on This Page — Do Not Cut or Separate Forms on This Page [7]

---
[7] Source: Internal Revenue Service

13. This example 1099 form was filled out by which of the following, and for which purpose?
   a) A corporation, to report payment made to an individual who did work for the corporation.
   b) An employee of a corporation to report his wages.
   c) A corporation, to report the wages paid to an employee.
   d) An individual, to report the income he earned doing work for a corporation.
   e) A corporation, to report a payment made to another corporation.

14. How much tax was withheld from Ronald Green throughout the year by Z Builders?
   a) $0.
   b) $500.
   c) $1000.
   d) $2500.
   e) $5500.

Questions 15 through 17 refer to the following excerpt of the Constitution:

Article I, Section 3 of the US Constitution:

> The Senate of the United States shall be composed of two Senators from each State, chosen by the Legislature thereof for six Years; and each Senator shall have one Vote.
>
> Immediately after they shall be assembled in Consequence of the first Election, they shall be divided as equally as may be into three Classes. The Seats of the Senators of the first Class shall be vacated at the Expiration of the second Year, of the second Class at the Expiration of the fourth Year, and of the third Class at the Expiration of the sixth Year, so that one third may be chosen every second Year; and if Vacancies happen by Resignation, or otherwise, during the Recess of the Legislature of any State, the Executive thereof may make temporary Appointments until the next Meeting of the Legislature, which shall then fill such Vacancies.
>
> No Person shall be a Senator who shall not have attained to the Age of thirty Years, and been nine Years a Citizen of the United States, and who shall not, when elected, be an Inhabitant of that State for which he shall be chosen.
>
> The Vice President of the United States shall be President of the Senate, but shall have no Vote, unless they are equally divided.
>
> The Senate shall choose their other Officers, and also a President pro tempore, in the Absence of the Vice President, or when he shall exercise the Office of President of the United States.
>
> The Senate shall have the sole Power to try all Impeachments. When sitting for that Purpose, they shall be on Oath or Affirmation. When the President of the United States is tried, the Chief Justice shall preside: And no Person shall be convicted without the Concurrence of two thirds of the Members present.

Judgment in Cases of Impeachment shall not extend further than to removal from Office, and disqualification to hold and enjoy any Office of honor, Trust or Profit under the United States: but the Party convicted shall nevertheless be liable and subject to Indictment, Trial, Judgment and Punishment, according to Law.

15. Of the following people, who would not be eligible to serve in the Senate based on the information given?
    a) A 28 year old man.
    b) A 42 year old woman.
    c) A person elected to serve as a Senator for Wisconsin, who was living in Washington DC during the election year.
    d) A person who was not born in the United States.
    e) A person who obtained US Citizenship in the 1980s.

16. Every two years, what happens in the Senate?
    a) The Senate tries an impeachment.
    b) The Vice President is allowed to vote with the Senate.
    c) The Senate is comprised of entirely new people.
    d) One-half of the Senate is up for re-election.
    e) One-third of the Senate seats are vacated and refilled by state elections.

17. Which of the following best describes the Vice President's role in the Senate?
    a) The Vice President acts as a member of the Senate.
    b) The Vice President is not allowed to attend Senate hearings.
    c) The Vice President presides over the Senate during impeachment trials.
    d) The Vice President presides over Senate sessions and breaks ties in Senate votes.
    e) The Vice President presides over Senate sessions but is never allowed to vote.

Questions 18 and 19 are based on the following information:

In 1913, the United States government created the Federal Reserve System, partially in response to financial panics in the years prior. The Federal Reserve System is tasked with using monetary policy to help the United States weather economic fluctuations, maintain employment rates, and keep inflation to a predictable rate. The Act of Congress that established the system ensured that while high-ranking members of the Federal Reserve Board are appointed by the President and confirmed by the Senate, the Federal Reserve is able to make decisions about monetary policy without approval by the branches of government.

18. Which of the following outcomes is prevented by giving the Federal Reserve System decision-making power independent of the branches of government?
    a) The Federal Reserve System using monetary policy to prevent high inflation.
    b) The President of the United States appointing the chairman of the Federal Reserve System.
    c) The Federal Reserve System using monetary policy to help the government create funds.
    d) The Federal Reserve System preventing financial panics.
    e) The Senate from approving the appointment of a board member to the Federal Reserve.

19. The responsibilities of the Federal Reserve System include all of the following *except*:
   a) Managing inflation rates.
   b) Appointing members to the Federal Reserve Board.
   c) Preventing high rises in the unemployment rate.
   d) Making decisions regarding monetary policy.
   e) Preventing financial panics.

Questions 20 through 22 are based on the following table and information:

Significant Inventions in Textile Production During the Industrial Revolution

Year	Invention	Effect on productivity
1733	**Flying Shuttle** – A device that allows one worker to weave across a wide loom quickly	Estimated to have doubled the productivity of one weaver
1764	**Spinning Jenny** – A device that allows one worker to produce several spools of yarn at one time, using a frame operated by a wheel.	At first, workers could spin 8 spools of yarn at once rather than 1. As the technology improved, this went up to as many as 120 spools at once.
1764	**Water Frame** – Another device used for spinning multiple spools of thread at once, the water frame used power sufficient enough to produce high-quality threads.	With the introduction of the water frame, both the warp and the weft threads needed for making cotton cloth could now be produced by fully mechanized means.
1779	**Spinning Mule** – This combined the technologies of the spinning jenny and the water frame, allowing higher-quality threads to be produced.	The cloth produced with the spinning mule was able to compete with higher-quality, more costly hand-made fabrics.

As the process of spinning thread and weaving cloth became more mechanized and more profitable, the lives of workers changed considerably. Many who worked in the textile industry were women, who were now earning more than male laborers in textile centers in Great Britain. However, the higher wages for these workers came along with longer hours and more dangerous conditions: many spent 12-14 hour shifts in hot and crowded factories, inhaling cotton fibers and using untested equipment. Many textile mills also employed children during this time period.

20. A worker who produced 10 spools of thread per day in 1760 would have produced how many spools of thread per day immediately after the invention of the spinning jenny?
   a) 10.
   b) 20.
   c) 40.
   d) 80.
   e) 100.

21. Each of these devices was invented in Great Britain. Which of the following is a likely effect these inventions had on that nation's economy?
   a) Great Britain began to export more cloth to the rest of the world.
   b) Great Britain lost workers due to the new technology.
   c) Cloth production went down.
   d) Worker productivity sank.
   e) Worker wages were reduced.

22. The passage explains which shifts in the lives of textile workers during the 1700s?
   a) They tended to work fewer hours and earn higher wages.
   b) They faced more dangerous tasks and earned lower wages.
   c) They became more productive and learned to use new machinery.
   d) They earned higher wages but faced more dangerous conditions.
   e) Their working conditions improved as they unionized.

Questions 23 and 24 are based on the map and information below:

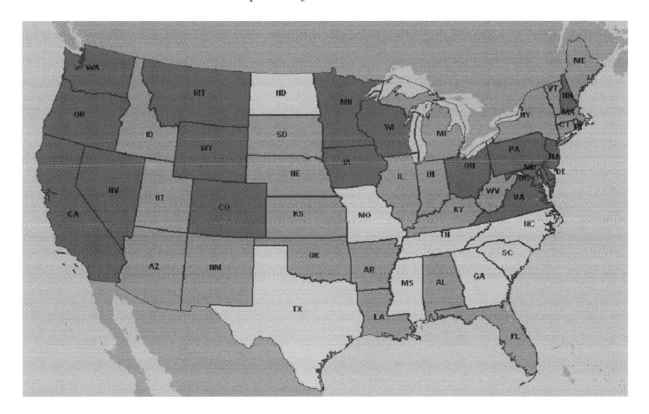

Registered Voters That Voted 2004
Source: United States Census Bureau

Percentage of Registered Voters That Voted

- 90.1 or Greater
- 85.1 - 90.0
- 80.1 - 85.0
- 70.1 - 80.0
- 60.1 - 70.0
- 60.0 or Less

In 2004, approximately 70% of registered voters nationwide voted in the federal election.

Nationwide, approximately 55% of those who were of eligible voting age voted in the 2004 federal election.

23. In how many states did fewer than 80% of registered voters vote in the federal election in 2004?

    a) 6.
    b) 8.
    c) 11.
    d) 14.
    e) 20.

24. In 2004, which of the following categories is the largest?

    a) Percentage of registered voters in Texas (TX) who voted.
    b) Percentage of registered voters in California (CA) who voted.
    c) Percentage of those of voting age in Texas who voted.
    d) Percentage of those of voting age in California who voted.
    e) Percentage of registered voters nationwide who voted.

Questions 25 and 26 are based on the following poster and information:

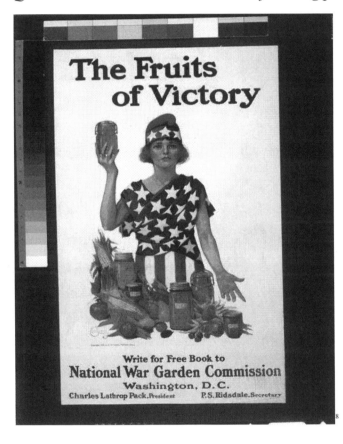

The poster to the left was used in 1918 in the United States to promote the concept of a Victory Garden. During World War I, food shortages became a problem in the United States and many other countries, as those who worked in agriculture enlisted in military service and food production regions in Europe became battlegrounds.

To address food shortages domestically, citizens were encouraged to plant their own vegetables at home or in public spaces such as parks. Tending to these gardens gave those at home a way to support the military effort and to combat the very real threat of food shortages.

Victory gardens came to the forefront again during World War II, especially when the forced internment of over 100,000 Japanese-Americans drastically reduced the agricultural capacity of the American West.

25. What was the purpose of the poster shown above?

    a) To promote the idea of Victory Gardens.
    b) To teach people how to plant a Victory Garden.
    c) To encourage people to enlist in military service.
    d) To boost morale of the public during WWI.
    e) To hide the dangers of food shortage.

---

[8] Image Source: Library of Congress Prints and Photographs Division Washington, D.C.

26. During which period were Japanese-Americans forced into internment camps?
   a) Before World War I.
   b) During World War I.
   c) The period between World War I and World War II.
   d) During World War II.
   e) After World War II.

Questions 27 through 29 are based on the map and information below:

Kyoto Protocol participation map, 2013-2020:

- Parties; Annex I & II countries with binding targets.
- Parties; Developing countries without binding targets.
- States not Party to the Protocol.
- Signatory country with no intention to ratify the treaty, with no binding targets.
- Countries that have denounced the Protocol, with no binding targets.
- Parties with no binding targets in the second period, which previously had targets.

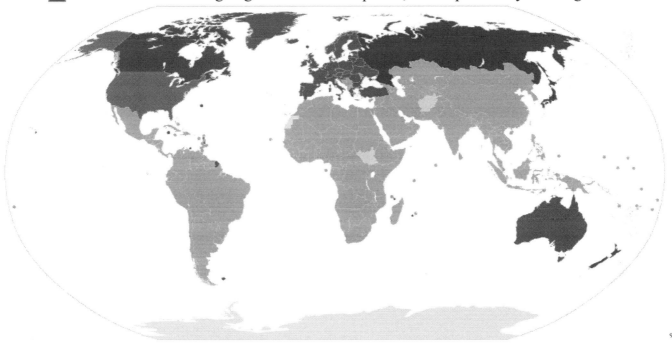

The Kyoto Protocol is an international treaty intended to address the emissions of greenhouse gases into the atmosphere. The Protocol was passed by the United Nations in 1997 and went into effect in 2005. The treaty has different restrictions for different nations which have ratified it: Annex I countries agreed to reduce greenhouse gas emissions by 5.2% before 2012. Developing countries which ratified the treaty were not held to any binding targets due to the difficulty of upholding them and the importance of prioritizing economic, health, and educational initiatives above environmental ones. However, many of these ratifying nations do attempt to limit emissions while growing their economies.

---

[9] Source: Wikimedia Commons, URL: http://en.wikipedia.org/wiki/Kyoto_Protocol

27. The majority of countries which have signed the Kyoto Treaty fall within which group?
   a) Annex I or Annex II.
   b) Developing countries.
   c) Countries which signed but did not ratify the treaty.
   d) Countries exempt from binding targets in the second period of the treaty.
   e) Countries which signed and then later denounced the treaty.

28. Which is the only country that signed the Kyoto Protocol with no intention of ratifying the treaty?
   a) Canada.
   b) Mexico.
   c) Australia.
   d) The United States.
   e) Russia.

29. Why was the Kyoto Protocol structured to allow different nations to have different targets in upholding the treaty?
   a) Countries in the north had higher greenhouse gas emissions in the first place.
   b) Structuring the treaty this way made it possible for every country to ratify the treaty.
   c) Placing no environmental restrictions on developing countries allows those countries to focus on other things.
   d) Some countries have denounced the Kyoto Protocol.
   e) The targets were meant to be realistic given the sizes of the different countries.

IN THE RUBBER COILS.
Scene—The Congo "Free" State.
[10]

Questions 30 through 31 are based on the political cartoon and information below:

In 1885, King Leopold of Belgium declared the Congo, the largest state in the African continent, to be his colony, called the Congo Free State. The territory remained under his control until 1908, and during that time Leopold used his power to brutally extract natural resources, including rubber, ivory, and mined minerals.

In 1908, public outrage over the treatment of the Congolese people led Belgium to annex the Congo as a colony of the state, leaving it no longer under the control of one man. The Congo remained a colony of Belgium until 1960, when it gained independence and was renamed the Republic of the Congo.

[10] Artist Linley Sambourne. Published in Punch Magazine November 1906.

30. The snake in the cartoon above is depicting who or what?
- a) The Belgian government.
- b) King Leopold.
- c) The rubber companies.
- d) Public outrage.
- e) The king of France.

31. The artist who drew this cartoon likely believed that:
- a) The Congolese people were suffering as a result of the extraction of resources.
- b) Mortality due to snake bites was a significant problem in the Congo.
- c) The Congo Free State should not belong to Belgium.
- d) The Republic of the Congo could benefit economically from producing rubber.
- e) People should boycott the rubber trade.

Questions 32 through 34 are based on the information in the following table:

Year	Act	Description
1789	United States Constitution, Article III	Establishes that all crimes, with the exception of impeachment cases, must be tried by a jury in the state in which they were committed.
1791	Bill of Rights, 6th Amendment	Requires that each individual member of a jury be unbiased, or without preconceptions, toward the defendant. To ensure that bias does not exist, both the prosecution and the defense sides of a trial have the chance to interview prospective jurors and eliminate those whom they find to have a bias.
1968	Jury Selection and Service Act	A comprehensive reform of the jury selection process, this act made every district court in the US compile names of potential jurors from voter registration lists or voting records. These lists could be supplemented by other means if they did not accurately reflect the demographics (age, race, gender) of the community.

32. Which of the following rights of those on trial was guaranteed by the Jury Selection and Service Act?
- a) The trial must occur in the state in which the crime was committed.
- b) The trial jury must be unbiased.
- c) The jury must be composed to reflect the demographics of the community.
- d) The defense has the opportunity to eliminate jurors whom they find to be biased before the trial begins.
- e) The trial must be decided by a jury.

33. The United States Declaration of Independence, adopted in 1776, denounced the British monarchy for often denying its subjects a trial by jury for accused crimes. Which of the following acts seeks to address this?
    a) Article III of the Constitution.
    b) The 6th Amendment in the Bill of Rights.
    c) The Jury Selection and Service Act.
    d) None of the above.

34. To uphold the Jury Selection and Service Act, what would a District Court need to do if its voter registration lists did not accurately reflect the population of people between the ages of 18 and 22 living in the district?
    a) Move all trials with defendants between the ages of 18 and 22 to another District Court.
    b) Interview all prospective jurors to ensure that they are unbiased.
    c) Decide the cases by the decision of the judge rather than by a jury.
    d) Cancel all trials in the District Court.
    e) Supplement the list of potential jurors by other means to include younger people.

Questions 35 and 36 are based on the following graph and information:

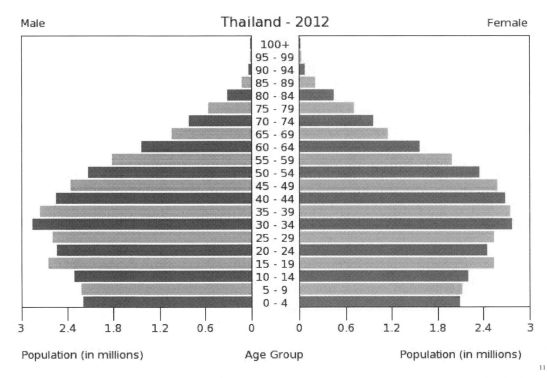

The horizontal axis of the population pyramid shows the population in millions of Thailand in 2012. The male population is shown on the left, in blue, and the female population is shown on the right, in red. Along the vertical axis, the populations of both genders are shown grouped by age, with the youngest populations shown at the bottom of the pyramid and the oldest at the top. The pyramid shows demographic trends in Thailand and can give information about the future composition of the Thai society.

[11] Source: The CIA World Factbook – Thailand. Public domain.

35. Which of the following groups of the Thai population was the largest in 2012?
    a) Males and females over the age of 80.
    b) Males between the ages of 15 and 19.
    c) Males between the ages of 30 and 34.
    d) Females under the age of 5.
    e) Females between the ages of 30 and 34.

36. Based on the data given in the pyramid, what will be different about Thai society in 2022?
    a) There will be more people aged 40-50 than people aged 30-40.
    b) Elementary schools serving students aged 5-10 will be more crowded than they were in 2012.
    c) There will be more women than men in the general population.
    d) The majority of workers will be within five years of the retirement age of 65.
    e) The birth rate will continue to decline.

Questions 37 through 39 are based on the following editorials:

A local newspaper recently ran an article explaining that the United States and the European Union were getting closer to creating a free trade agreement, which would lower the taxes paid on products and materials shipped between the two regions. Two people wrote to the paper to respond to the article:

Letter 1	Letter 2
Dear Editor,	Dear Editor,
I am concerned about this proposed free trade agreement between the United States and the 27 countries in the European Union. The North American Free Trade Agreement, between the United States, Canada, and Mexico, makes more sense to me because we are all neighbors and we do not produce the same types of goods, so there is less competition and more reason to trade. However, for example in Germany auto manufacturing is a big industry. If we remove the taxes from imported cars, fewer people will buy American-made cars because German cars will become cheaper than they are now. This hurts our domestic industries. My son works in an auto plant, and if demand for American cars goes down, he could lose his job.	I'm writing because I manage a small clothing business, and a free-trade agreement between the US and the EU would positively impact my bottom line. I design swimsuits and other garments, which are mostly manufactured in the Czech Republic due to their strong garment manufacturing abilities. When I ship the raw materials to them and then when they ship the finished products back to me, we are taxed twice and this raises the prices of my clothes. Then, through online sales, we ship some clothes to countries in the EU – and they are taxed again. Eliminating this triple tax means that my clothes will have a lower final price for everyone. This must be true for lots of businesses, so the free trade agreement would mean cheaper consumer goods for all.

37. Which of the following is a fact about a free-trade agreement between the United States and the European Union?
    a) It would lower the prices of consumer goods for everyone.
    b) It would cause American workers to lose their jobs.
    c) It would affect every country on the European continent.
    d) It would lower tax revenue for the United States government.
    e) It would eliminate the taxes on goods that are imported to the EU from the US.

38. The author of Letter 1 compares the proposed free trade agreement to what?
    a) The American auto industry.
    b) The global garment market.
    c) The North American Free Trade Agreement.
    d) The European Union.
    e) The United Nations.

39. Which of the following accurately describes the production chain that the author of Letter 2 uses in his or her argument?
    a) Swimsuits are designed and manufactured in the Czech Republic, and then shipped to the United States where they are purchased and shipped to customers in countries in the European Union.
    b) Swimsuits are designed in the United States, manufactured in the European Union, and then shipped back to the United States, where they are sold or shipped to customers in the European Union.
    c) Swimsuits are designed in the United Kingdom, manufactured in the Czech Republic, and then shipped to the United States to be sold.
    d) Swimsuits are designed and manufactured in the United States, and then shipped to customers in the Czech Republic and other countries in the European Union.
    e) Swimsuits are designed in the United States, manufactured in the European Union, and then sold to customers in the European Union.

Questions 40 and 41 use information from the following historical map and information:

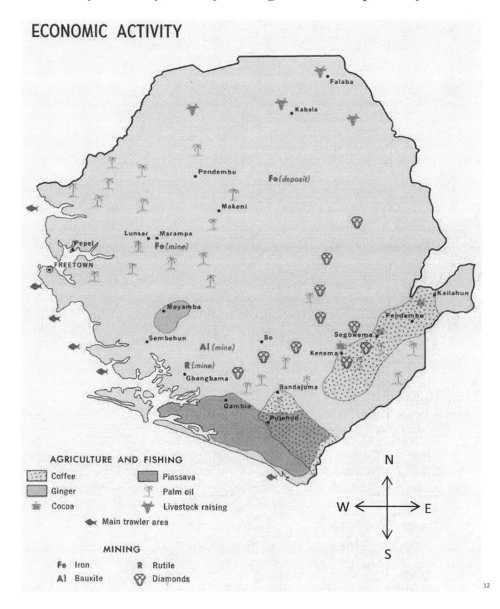

The above map shows the major sources of economic activity in Sierra Leone, in western Africa, in the year 1969, nine years after its independence from Great Britain.

40. Most of the mining activity in Sierra Leone in the 1960s occurred where?
    a) In the north part of the country.
    b) In the south east part of the country.
    c) Along the western coast.
    d) Near Freetown.
    e) Near where livestock was raised.

---

[12] Source: Map produced by the United States CIA, stored at the University of Texas Perry Castañeda Library.

41. From the map, what can be inferred about the economy of Sierra Leone in the late 1960s?
   a) Livestock would become less important to the economy over time.
   b) Growing and harvesting ginger was not important to the economy.
   c) Manufacturing was not a large part of the economy.
   d) After independence from Britain, the economy grew significantly.
   e) Harvesting palm oil was lucrative.

Questions 42 and 43 refer to the following passage:

The case of the Massachusetts Commonwealth versus Ferdinando Nicola Sacco and Bartolomeo Vanzetti first went to trial in 1920, but it is still controversial today. Sacco and Vanzetti, two Italian immigrants to the United States, were convicted of robbing the payroll of a factory and of attempted murder. The convictions rested on evidence that seemed inconclusive, such as conflicting eyewitness accounts. However, anti-immigrant sentiments in the jury and Sacco and Vanzetti's participation in local anarchist groups might have influenced the convictions.

Sacco and Vanzetti appealed to the Supreme Court, which upheld their convictions in 1926. Both men were executed by the state in 1927. Legal historians have since interpreted the case as an example of the government denying civil liberties to citizens in order to put a stop to anti-government, anarchist political activity.

In 1977, the governor of Massachusetts, Michael Dukakis, ordered a report on whether the trial had been conducted fairly. Investigators found that the trail was not fair, so Dukakis issued a statement that Sacco and Vanzetti should have all "disgrace" removed from their names.

42. According to the passage, what might have unjustly influenced the convictions of Ferdinando Sacco and Bartolomeo Vanzetti?
   a) Eyewitness accounts.
   b) Immigration laws.
   c) Their lack of participation in local anarchist groups.
   d) Their lack of representation by competent lawyers.
   e) Anti-immigration sentiment.

43. Which of the following events happened third?
   a) Michael Dukakis commissioned a report on the trials of Sacco and Vanzetti.
   b) Sacco and Vanzetti were executed.
   c) A crime was committed, for which Sacco and Vanzetti were convicted.
   d) The Sacco and Vanzetti case went to the Supreme Court.
   e) The Sacco and Vanzetti case first went to trial.

Questions 44 through 46 are based on the timeline presented below:

August 6, 1945	The United States begins bombing Japanese cities Hiroshima and Nagasaki with atomic weapons during World War II.
March 5, 1946	British Prime Minister Winston Churchill gives his famous speech warning of the "Iron Curtain" of Communism falling across Europe, separating former allies: the Soviet Union and its satellites from the rest of Europe.
March 12, 1946	U.S. President Harry Truman announces his foreign policy plan of giving monetary aid to Greece and Turkey to prevent them from falling under Soviet control.
June 4, 1947	U.S. Secretary of State George Marshall announces his foreign policy plan of giving aid to all war-ravaged countries in Western Europe to prevent the spread of Soviet Communism.
August 29, 1949	The Soviet Union successfully tests its first atomic bomb, becoming the second world power with nuclear capability.

44. What event must have happened between August 6, 1945 and March 5, 1946?
   a) The United States tested its first atomic bomb.
   b) The Marshall Plan was announced.
   c) The Soviet Union began to exert influence over its satellite countries.
   d) World War II ended.
   e) Communism began to spread to Greece and Turkey.

45. During the 1940s, the primary way that the United States worked to contain communism through diplomacy involved what?
   a) Constructing the Iron Curtain.
   b) Giving aid to other countries.
   c) Testing nuclear weapons.
   d) Declaring war on the Soviet Union.
   e) Announcing that the Soviet Union as an ally.

46. For how many years was there only one world power with nuclear capabilities?
   a) 1.
   b) 2.
   c) 3.
   d) 4.
   e) 5.

Questions 47 and 48 are based on the following map and information:

The map above shows the time zone boundaries in South America. The Earth is divided into 24 time zones, so that the hour increases as a person moves east from the Prime Meridian, a longitude line that runs north to south through Greenwich, Great Britain. South America, shown above, lies in the time zones which are 5 hours, 4 hours, 3 hours, and 2 hours earlier than the hour at the Prime Meridian. For example, if it was 8:00 pm in Greenwich, it would be 4:00 pm in Bolivia, which lies in the -4 time zone. Time zone boundaries are shown in red, and they vary from the longitudinal lines so that the citizens of a country or region can all be on the same clock. For example, Argentinian leaders chose to be in the same time zone as eastern Brazil for business reasons, even though Argentina lies mostly in the next time zone over.

[13] Source: CIA World Factbook, excerpted from the map *Standard Time Zones of the World*

47. If it is 9:00 am in São Paulo, Brazil, what time is it in Bogotá, Columbia?

    a) 7:00 am.
    b) 8:00 am.
    c) 9:00 am.
    d) 10:00 am.
    e) 11:00 am.

48. Which of the following countries is divided into multiple time zones?

    a) Chile.
    b) Peru.
    c) Venezuela.
    d) Brazil.
    e) Argentina.

Questions 49 and 50 are based on the following passage:

The World Bank was established in 1944 during the Bretton Woods Conference about international financial health. The World Bank, as an institution, is intended to combat global poverty by assisting developing countries with loans for programs that will benefit their citizens. In 1994, the World Bank together with the International Monetary Fund began a program to help 39 countries, which are classified as heavily indebted and poor, to cancel out their debt.

Critics of the World Bank say that it attaches too many strings to the aid it gives: for example, to qualify for a World Bank loan, many countries in sub-Saharan Africa had to undergo what was called "structural adjustment." This included a series of policies that required countries' state-owned resources to be sold to private companies and their expensive government-run social programs to be cut. While the structural adjustment policies are well-intended to create economic growth, when they are implemented too quickly or without proper support they can actually create economic depressions instead.

49. What is the stated purpose of the World Bank?

    a) To implement structural adjustment policies.
    b) To cancel out the debt of developing countries.
    c) To combat global poverty.
    d) To give loans to private companies.
    e) To sell state-owned resources to private companies.

50. Which of the following actions of the World Bank would a critic of the World Bank use as an example of a harmful policy?

    a) Loaning $60 million to Rwanda to increase electricity access.
    b) Giving Nicaragua a structural adjustment credit for selling state-owned assets to foreign investors.
    c) Loaning money to Lebanon for the purpose of hiring unemployed young people in government roles.
    d) Investing in green-energy experimental facilities in rural China.
    e) Funding a program to enforce wastewater treatment regulations in industrialized areas of Vietnam.

Test Your Knowledge: Social Studies – Answers

1. **c)**. The passage lists at least three states that were formed from land acquired in the Louisiana Purchase – Louisiana, Montana, and Mississippi. The Purchase included land that would become part of 15 states.

2. **a)**. Based on the passage, it was controversial because there was debate about whether it was Constitutional. Answers **b)** and **c)** were not addressed in the passage, and **d)** and **e)** would be reasons to support the purchase.

3. **d)**. The cartoon was published during the long ratification process, which would be between June 1919 and August 1920.

4. **c)**. The passage states that 36 states were needed; the last three buttons are labeled: "34, 35, 36."

5. **e)**. "Our methods of defense ought to improve with our increase of property."

6. **c)**. All other answers are mentioned in the passage.

7. **a)**. All other statements can be refuted from lines in the passage.

8. **b)**. This time span shows the longest decline on the graph.

9. **c)**. This would increase production, which is shown on the graph at 1933.

10. **c)**.

11. **d)**. The highway stretches across the country and through most major cities. The other statements are all false: San Juan de Manapiare is not close to anything; Venezuela has no railroads; Bogota is the capital of Columbia, and Bogota and Caracas are closer to 600 miles apart.

12. **d)**. North of the river contains almost all of the cities in the country, where 95% of Venezuelans live.

13. **a)**. This 1099 form is filled out by a corporation which is paying an individual, not an employee, for work done.

14. **a)**. None of the boxes indicating taxes withheld show a dollar amount.

15. **a)**. Senators must be at least 30 years old.

16. **e)**. The second paragraph of Article 3 explains that every two years, one-third of Senators end their terms.

17. **d)**. The fourth paragraph explains the role of the VP.

18. **c)**. The intention is to prevent the government from manipulating the Federal Reserve into enacting policy that only helps those in power.

19. **b)**. The board members are appointed by the President.

20. d). At first, the spinning jenny allowed a worker to produce 8 spools of thread at once.

21. a). As cloth production was more efficient, the country exported more cloth

22. d). The passage explains that textile workers were earning more money but facing dangerous and unpleasant working conditions.

23. b). 8 states are shaded light green to indicate less than 80% registered voter turnout.

24. b). In California, the percentage of registered voters who voted was higher than the same in Texas or the nationwide average. Also, for all states, the percentage of registered voters who voted was higher than the percentage of those of voting age who voted.

25. a). The poster does not teach how to plant the garden, but it does encourage people to learn more about the concept. Boosting morale may be another effect, but is not the primary purpose of this poster.

26. d). Found in the third paragraph of the passage.

27. b). These are the light green countries shown on the map.

28. d). The only orange country on the map is the United States.

29. c). As stated in the passage, developing countries were exempted from the restrictions so that they could focus on other goals, like improving education and healthcare.

30. b). King Leopold, shown with the crown on the head of the snake, was the one viewed as responsible for what was happening in the Congo.

31. a). The brutality of the rubber trade was causing a public outrage leading up to 1908. Answer **b)** is wrong, because the snake is a symbol, not the actual problem. Answer **c)** is wrong, because there was not a public outrage over the colonization, and the solution to the problem of the brutality was seen as annexing the colony to Belgium rather than letting it be owned by King Leopold independently. Answers **d)** and **e)** are not drawn from the passage.

32. c). The Selection and Service Act was written to ensure that juries were composed to reflect the community they serve.

33. a). Article II guarantees that all crimes will be tried by a jury, with the exception of impeachment cases.

34. e). As explained in the table. Answer **b)** is covered by the Bill of Rights, **c)** is unconstitutional, and **a)** and **d)** are not mentioned anywhere in the table.

35. c). This one bar totals nearly 3 million, and is larger than all the other groups given, even those that are adding several bars from the pyramid.

36. a). The bars representing people in their 30s were the longest in 2012. In 2022, those people will be in their forties. Answers **b), d),** and **e)** cannot be supported by the graph. Answer **c)** may be true in 2022, but it was true in 2012 so it is not a difference.

37. e). This is the only fact we can tell from the articles. Answers **a), b),** and **d)** are conclusions people can make from this fact, but they are not known for sure. Answer **c)** is wrong; it would only directly affect the countries in the EU which is not every country.

38. c). In the first paragraph, this comparison is made.

39. b). This best fits the description of the process given in the letter. The Czech Republic is in the European Union, which we know because the writer of the letter says that the free-trade agreement would eliminate the taxes on products and materials shipped from the US to the manufacturer in the Czech Republic.

40. b).

41. The map shows livestock, fishing, mining, and agriculture as the important components of the economy; there is nothing about manufacturing. Answer **b)** is wrong, because we cannot tell how much money is brought in by ginger just from the size of the area where it is grown. Answers **a)** and **d)** are wrong, because we have no reference of the size of the economy prior to 1960 or after 1969. Answer **e)** is wrong, because we cannot tell that from the map.

42. e). This answer is found at the end of the first paragraph in the passage.

43. d). The correct order is **c), e), d), b),** and **a).**

44. d). The events of August 6, 1945 triggered the end of World War II. By March 5, the Soviet Union and Western Europe are described as "former allies" – no longer on the same side, as they were in WWII.

45. b). The Truman and Marshall Plans both involved giving aid to countries at risk of becoming under Soviet influence.

46. d). From 1945 to 1949, the United States was the only global power with nuclear weapons.

47. a). Bogotá is two time zones to the west of São Paulo, so it will be two hours earlier there.

48. d). Brazil uses the -3 time zone in the east and the -4 time zone in the west because it is so large.

49. c). As found in the first paragraph

50. b). The criticism mentioned in the passage is of the structural adjustment policies, which can open up developing countries to new problems.

Chapter 4: Mathematics

Before you take the TASC test, you want to make sure that you have a good understanding of those math areas which will be covered. You will need to sharpen your skills – and we'll provide you with the knowledge that you'll need for the test.

Math Concepts Tested

You have a much better chance of getting a good score if you know what to expect. The test covers math up to and including the first semester of Algebra II, as well as fundamental geometry. You will not be given any formulas, such as those required for geometric calculations, so make sure to study them until they are solidified concepts in your mind.

Here is a breakdown of areas covered:

Numbers and Operations
- Absolute values, inequalities, probabilities, exponents, and radicals.

Algebra and Functions
- Basic equation-solving, simultaneous equations, binomials & polynomials, and inequalities.

Geometry and Measurement
- Angle relationships, area and perimeter of geometric shapes, and volume.

Statistics and Probability
- Finding the statistical probability or chances of something happening

Math skills that you won't need:

- Working with bulky numbers or endless calculations.
- Working with imaginary numbers or the square roots of negative numbers.
- Trigonometry or calculus.

The Most Common Mistakes

People make mistakes all the time – but during a test, those mistakes can cost you a passing score. Watch out for these common mistakes that people make:

- Answering with the wrong sign (positive / negative).

- Mixing up the Order of Operations.

- Misplacing a decimal.

- Not reading the question thoroughly (and therefore providing an answer that was not asked for.)

- Circling the wrong letter, or filling in wrong circle choice.

If you're thinking, "Those ideas are just common sense" – exactly! Most of the mistakes made are simple mistakes. Regardless, they still result in a wrong answer and the loss of a potential point.

Helpful Strategies

1. **Go Back to the Basics**: First and foremost, practice your basic skills: sign changes, order of operations, simplifying fractions, and equation manipulation. These are the skills used most on the test, though they are applied in different contexts. Remember that when it comes right down to it, all math problems rely on the four basic skills of addition, subtraction, multiplication, and division. All that changes is the order in which they are used to solve a problem.

2. **Don't Rely on Mental Math**: Using mental math is great for eliminating answer choices, but ALWAYS WRITE IT DOWN! This cannot be stressed enough. Use whatever paper is provided; by writing and/or drawing out the problem, you are more likely to catch any mistakes. The act of writing things down forces you to organize your calculations, leading to an improvement in your score.

3. **The Three-Times Rule**:

   - **Step One – Read the question**: Write out the given information.

   - **Step Two – Read the question**: Set up your equation(s) and solve.

   - **Step Three – Read the question:** Make sure that your answer makes sense (is the amount too large or small; is the answer in the correct unit of measure; etc.).

4. **Make an Educated Guess**: Eliminate those answer choices which you are relatively sure are incorrect, and then guess from the remaining choices. Educated guessing is critical to increasing your score.

Math Formulas, Facts, and Terms that You Need to Know

The next few pages will cover the various math subjects (starting with the basics, but in no particular order) along with worked examples. Use this guide to determine the areas in which you need more review and work these areas first. You should take your time at first and let your brain recall the math necessary to solve the problems, using the examples given to remember these skills.

Order of Operations

PEMDAS – **P**arentheses/**E**xponents/**M**ultiply/**D**ivide/**A**dd/**S**ubtract

Perform the operations within parentheses first, and then any exponents. After those steps, perform all multiplication and division. (These are done from left to right, as they appear in the problem) Finally, do all required addition and subtraction, also from left to right as they appear in the problem.

> **Example**: Solve $(-(2)^2 - (4 + 7))$.
> $(-4 - 11) = -\mathbf{15}$.
>
> **Example**: Solve $((5)^2 \div 5 + 4 * 2)$.
> $25 \div 5 + 4 * 2$.
>
> $5 + 8 = \mathbf{13}$.

Positive & Negative Number Rules

(+) + (-) = Subtract the two numbers. Solution gets the sign of the larger number.

(-) + (-) = Negative number.

(-) * (-) = Positive number.

(-) * (+) = Negative number.

(-) / (-) = Positive number.

(-) / (+) = Negative number.

Greatest Common Factor (GCF)

The greatest factor that divides two numbers.

> **Example**: The GCF of 24 and 18 is 6. 6 is the largest number, or greatest factor, that can divide both 24 and 18.

Geometric Sequence

Each term is equal to the previous term multiplied by x.

> **Example**: 2, 4, 8, 16.
>
> $x = \mathbf{2}$.

Fractions

Adding and subtracting fractions requires a common denominator.

Find a common denominator for:

$$\frac{2}{3} - \frac{1}{5}$$

$$\frac{2}{3} - \frac{1}{5} = \frac{2}{3}\left(\frac{5}{5}\right) - \frac{1}{5}\left(\frac{3}{3}\right) = \frac{10}{15} - \frac{3}{15} = \frac{7}{15}$$

To add mixed fractions, work first the whole numbers, and then the fractions.

$$2\frac{1}{4} + 1\frac{3}{4} = 3\frac{4}{4} = \mathbf{4}$$

To subtract mixed fractions, convert to single fractions by multiplying the whole number by the denominator and adding the numerator. Then work as above.

$$2\frac{1}{4} - 1\frac{3}{4} = \frac{9}{4} - \frac{7}{4} = \frac{2}{4} = \frac{1}{2}$$

To multiply fractions, convert any mixed fractions into single fractions and multiply across; reduce to lowest terms if needed.

$$2\frac{1}{4} * 1\frac{3}{4} = \frac{9}{4} * \frac{7}{4} = \frac{63}{16} = 3\frac{15}{16}$$

To divide fractions, convert any mixed fractions into single fractions, flip the second fraction, and then multiply across.

$$2\frac{1}{4} \div 1\frac{3}{4} = \frac{9}{4} \div \frac{7}{4} = \frac{9}{4} * \frac{4}{7} = \frac{36}{28} = 1\frac{8}{28} = 1\frac{2}{7}$$

Probabilities

A probability is found by dividing the number of desired outcomes by the number of possible outcomes. (The piece divided by the whole.)

Example: What is the probability of picking a blue marble if 3 of the 15 marbles are blue?

3/15 = 1/5. The probability is **1 in 5** that a blue marble is picked.

Prime Factorization

Expand to prime number factors.

Example: 104 = 2 * 2 * 2 * 13.

Absolute Value

The absolute value of a number is its distance from zero, not its value.

So in $|x| = a$, "x" will equal "$-a$" as well as "a."

Likewise, $|3| = 3$, and $|-3| = 3$.

Equations with absolute values will have two answers. Solve each absolute value possibility separately. All solutions must be checked into the original equation.

> **Example:** Solve for x:
> $|2x - 3| = x + 1$.
>
> Equation One: $2x - 3 = -(x + 1)$.
> $\quad\quad\quad\quad\quad 2x - 3 = -x - 1$.
> $\quad\quad\quad\quad\quad 3x = 2$.
> $\quad\quad\quad\quad\quad x = 2/3$.
>
> Equation Two: $2x - 3 = x + 1$.
> $\quad\quad\quad\quad\quad x = 4$.

Mean, Median, Mode

Mean is a math term for "average." Total all terms and divide by the number of terms.

Find the mean of 24, 27, and 18.

$24 + 27 + 18 = 69 \div 3 = \mathbf{23}$.

Median is the middle number of a given set, found after the numbers have all been put in numerical order. In the case of a set of even numbers, the middle two numbers are averaged.

What is the median of 24, 27, and 18?

18, **24**, 27.

What is the median of 24, 27, 18, and 19?

18, 19, 24, 27 ($19 + 24 = 43$. $43/2 = \mathbf{21.5}$).

Mode is the number which occurs most frequently within a given set.

What is the mode of 2, 5, 4, 4, 3, 2, 8, 9, 2, 7, 2, and 2?

The mode would be **2** because it appears the most within the set.

Exponent Rules

Rule	Example
$x^0 = 1$	$5^0 = 1$
$x^1 = x$	$5^1 = 5$
$x^a \cdot x^b = x^{a+b}$	$5^2 * 5^3 = 5^5$
$(xy)^a = x^a y^a$	$(5 * 6)^2 = 5^2 * 6^2 = 25 * 36$
$(x^a)^b = x^{ab}$	$(5^2)^3 = 5^6$
$(x/y)^a = x^a/y^a$	$(10/5)^2 = 10^2/5^2 = 100/25$
$x^a/y^b = x^{a-b}$	$5^4/5^3 = 5^1 = 5$ (remember $x \neq 0$)
$x^{1/a} = \sqrt[a]{x}$	$25^{1/2} = \sqrt[2]{25} = 5$
$x^{-a} = \dfrac{1}{x^a}$	$5^{-2} = \dfrac{1}{5^2} = \dfrac{1}{25}$ (remember $x \neq 0$)
$(-x)^a$ = positive number if "a" is even; negative number if "a" is odd.	

Roots

Root of a Product: $\sqrt[n]{a \cdot b} = \sqrt[n]{a} \cdot \sqrt[n]{b}$

Root of a Quotient: $\sqrt[n]{\dfrac{a}{b}} = \dfrac{\sqrt[n]{a}}{\sqrt[n]{b}}$

Fractional Exponent: $\sqrt[n]{a^m} = a^{m/n}$

Literal Equations

Equations with more than one variable. Solve in terms of one variable first.

Example: Solve for y: $4x + 3y = 3x + 2y$.

Step 1 – Combine like terms: $3y - 2y = 4x - 2x$.

Step 2 – Solve for y: $y = 2x$.

Midpoint

To determine the midpoint between two points, simply add the two x coordinates together and divide by 2 (midpoint x). Then add the y coordinates together and divide by 2 (midpoint y).

$$\left(\frac{x_1 + x_2}{2}, \frac{y_1 + y}{2} \right)$$

Slope

The formula used to calculate the slope (m) of a straight line connecting two points is: $m = (y_2 - y_1) / (x_2 - x_1)$ = change in y / change in x.

Example: Calculate slope of the line in the diagram:

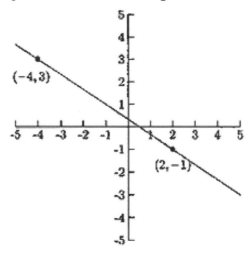

$m = (3 - (-1))/(-4 - 2) = 4/-6 = $ **- 2/3**.

Inequalities

Inequalities are solved like linear and algebraic equations, except the sign must be reversed when dividing by a negative number.

Example: $-7x + 2 < 6 - 5x$.

Step 1 – Combine like terms: $-2x < 4$.

Step 2 – Solve for x. (Reverse the sign): **$x > $-2.**

Solving compound inequalities will give you two answers.

Example: $-4 \leq 2x - 2 \leq 6$.

Step 1 – Add 2 to each term to isolate x: $-2 \leq 2x \leq 8$.

Step 2: Divide by 2: $-1 \leq x \leq 4$.

Solution set is **[-1, 4]**.

96

Algebraic Equations

When simplifying or solving algebraic equations, you need to be able to utilize all math rules: exponents, roots, negatives, order of operations, etc.

1. Add & Subtract: Only the coefficients of like terms.

   Example: $5xy + 7y + 2yz + 11xy - 5yz = 16xy + 7y - 3yz$.

2. Multiplication: First the coefficients then the variables.

   Example: Monomial * Monomial.

   $(3x^4y^2z)(2y^4z^5) = 6x^4y^6z^6$.

   (A variable with no exponent has an implied exponent of 1.)

   Example: Monomial * Polynomial.

   $(2y^2)(y^3 + 2xy^2z + 4z) = 2y^5 + 4xy^4z + 8y^2z$.

   Example: Binomial * Binomial.

   $(5x + 2)(3x + 3)$.

   (Remember FOIL – First, Outer, Inner, Last.)

   First: $5x * 3x = 15x^2$.

   Outer: $5x * 3 = 15x$.

   Inner: $2 * 3x = 6x$.

   Last: $2 * 3 = 6$.

   Combine like terms: $15x^2 + 21x + 6$.

   Example: Binomial * Polynomial.

   $(x + 3)(2x^2 - 5x - 2)$.

   First term: $x(2x^2 - 5x - 2) = 2x^3 - 5x^2 - 2x$.

   Second term: $3(2x^2 - 5x - 2) = 6x^2 - 15x - 6$.

   Added Together: $2x^3 + x^2 - 17x - 6$.

Distributive Property

When a variable is placed outside of a parenthetical set, it is *distributed* to all of the variables within that set.

$5(2y - 3x) = 10y - 15x$ [Can also be written as $(2y - 3x)5$].

$2x(3y + 1) + 6x = 6xy + 2x + 6x = 6xy + 8x$.

Combining Like Terms

This is exactly how it sounds! When a variable (x, y, z, r – anything!) is present in an equation, you can combine those terms with like variables.

$9r + 2r = 11r$.

$4x + 2y + 3 - 2x = 2x + 2y + 3$.

Arithmetic Sequence

Each term is equal to the previous term plus x.

Example: 2, 5, 8, 11.

$2 + 3 = 5; 5 + 3 = 8...$ etc.

$x = 3$.

Fundamental Counting Principle

(The number of possibilities of an event happening) * (the number of possibilities of another event happening) = the total number of possibilities.

Example: If you take a multiple choice test with 5 questions, with 4 answer choices for each question, how many test result possibilities are there?

Solution: Question 1 has 4 choices; question 2 has 4 choices; etc.

4 *4 * 4 * 4 * 4 (one for each question) = **1024 possible test results**.

Linear Systems

There are two different methods can be used to solve multiple equation linear systems:

- **Substitution method**: This solves for one variable in one equation and substitutes it into the other equation.

    Example: Solve: $3y - 4 + x = 0$ and $5x + 6y = 11$.

    1. Step 1: Solve for one variable:
        $3y - 4 = 0$.
        $3y + x = 4$.
        $x = 4 - 3y$.

    2. Step 2: Substitute into the second equation and solve:
        $5(4 - 3y) + 6y = 11$.
        $20 - 15y + 6y = 11$.
        $20 - 9y = 11$.
        $-9y = -9$.
        $y = 1$.

    3. Step 3: Substitute into the first equation:
        $3(1) - 4 + x = 0$.
        $-1 + x = 0$.
        $x = 1$.

        Solution: $x = 1, y = 1$.

- **Addition method**: Manipulate one of the equations so that when it is added to the other, one variable is eliminated.

    Example: Solve: $2x + 4y = 8$ and $4x + 2y = 10$.

    1. Step 1: Manipulate one equation to eliminate a variable when added together:
        $-2(2x + 4y = 8)$.
        $-4x - 8y = -16$.
        $(-4x - 8y = -16) + (4x + 2y = 10)$.
        $-6y = -6$.
        $y = 1$.

    2. Step 2: Plug into an equation to solve for the other variable:
        $2x + 4(1) = 8$.
        $2x + 4 = 8$.
        $2x = 4$.
        $x = 2$.

        Solution: $x = 2, y = 1$.

Quadratics

Factoring: Converting $ax^2 + bx + c$ to factored form. Find two numbers that are factors of c and whose sum is b.

Example: Factor: $2x^2 + 12x + 18 = 0$.

1. Step 1: If possible, factor out a common monomial:
    $2(x^2 - 6x + 9)$.

2. Step 2: Find two numbers that are factors of 9 and which equal -6 when added:
    $2(x \quad)(x \quad)$.
    $\quad$ -3 , -3

3. Step 3: Fill in the binomials. Be sure to check your answer signs.
    $2(x - 3)(x - 3)$.

4. Step 4: To solve, set each to equal 0.
    $x - 3 = 0$.
    So, $x = 3$.

Difference of squares:

$a^2 - b^2 = (a + b)(a - b)$.

$a^2 + 2ab + b^2 = (a + b)(a + b)$.

$a^2 - 2ab + b^2 = (a - b)(a - b)$.

Permutations

The number of ways a set number of items can be arranged. Recognized by the use of a factorial (n!), with n being the number of items.

If $n = 3$, then $3! = 3 * 2 * 1 = 6$. If you need to arrange n number of things but x number are alike, then n! is divided by x!

Example: How many different ways can the letters in the word **balance** be arranged?

Solution: There are 7 letters so *n!* = 7! and 2 letters are the same so *x!* = 2! Set up the equation:

$$\frac{7 * 6 * 5 * 4 * 3 * 2 * 1}{2 * 1} = \textbf{2540 ways}.$$

Combinations

To calculate total number of possible combinations use the formula:

n!/r! (n-r)!   n = # of objects   r = # of objects selected at a time

Example: If seven people are selected in groups of three, how many different combinations are possible?

Solution:

$$\frac{7 * 6 * 5 * 4 * 3 * 2 * 1}{(3 * 2 * 1)(7 - 3)} = \textbf{210 possible combinations.}$$

Know the Names of Sided Plane Figures:

- **3 Sides** – Triangle (or Trigon)

- **4 Sides** – Quadrilateral (or Tetragon)

- **5 Sides** – Pentagon

- **6 Sides** – Hexagon

- **7 Sides** – Heptagon

- **8 Sides** – Octagon

- **9 Sides** – Nonagon

- **10 Sides** – Decagon

- **11 Sides** – Hendecagon

- **12 Sides** – Dodecagon

- **13 Sides** Tridecagon

- **14 Sides** – Tetradecagon

- **15 Sides** – Pentadecagon

- **16 Sides** – Hexadecagon

- **17 Sides** – Heptadecagon

- **18 Sides** – Octadecagon

Geometry

- **Acute Angle**: Measures less than 90°.

- **Acute Triangle**: Each angle measures less than 90°.

- **Obtuse Angle**: Measures greater than 90°.

- **Obtuse Triangle**: One angle measures greater than 90°.

- **Adjacent Angles**: Share a side and a vertex.

- **Complementary Angles**: Adjacent angles that sum to 90°.

- **Supplementary Angles**: Adjacent angles that sum to 180°.

- **Vertical Angles**: Angles that are opposite of each other. They are always congruent (equal in measure).

- **Equilateral Triangle**: All angles are equal.

- **Isosceles Triangle**: Two sides and two angles are equal.

- **Scalene**: No equal angles.

- **Parallel Lines**: Lines that will never intersect. Y **ll** X means line Y is parallel to line X.

- **Perpendicular lines**: Lines that intersect or cross to form 90° angles.

- **Transversal Line**: A line that crosses parallel lines.

- **Bisector**: Any line that cuts a line segment, angle, or polygon exactly in half.

- **Polygon**: Any enclosed plane shape with three or more connecting sides (ex. a triangle).

- **Regular Polygon**: Has all equal sides and equal angles (ex. square).

- **Arc**: A portion of a circle's edge.

- **Chord**: A line segment that connects two different points on a circle.

- **Tangent**: Something that touches a circle at only one point without crossing through it.

- **Sum of Angles**: The sum of angles of a polygon can be calculated using $(n-1)180°$, when n = the number of sides.

Regular Polygons

Polygon Angle Principle: S = The sum of interior angles of a polygon with n-sides.

$S = (n - 2)180$.

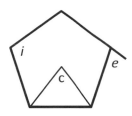

The measure of each central angle (c) is $360°/n$.
The measure of each interior angle (i) is $(n - 2)180°/n$.
The measure of each exterior angle (e) is $360°/n$.

To compare areas of similar polygons: $A_1/A_2 = (\text{side}_1/\text{side}_2)^2$.

Triangles

The angles in a triangle add up to $180°$.

Area of a triangle = $\frac{1}{2} * b * h$, or $\frac{1}{2}bh$.

Pythagoras' Theorem: $a^2 + b^2 = c^2$.

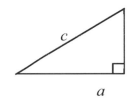

Trapezoids

Four-sided polygon, in which the bases (and only the bases) are parallel.
Isosceles Trapezoid – base angles are congruent.

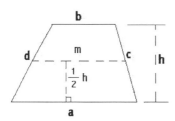

Area and Perimeter of a Trapezoid

$$m = \frac{1}{2}(a + b)$$

$$Area = \frac{1}{2}h * (a + b) = m * h$$

$$Perimeter = a + b + c + d = 2m + c + d$$

If m is the median then: $m \parallel \overline{AB}$ and $m \parallel \overline{CD}$

Rhombus

Four-sided polygon, in which all four sides are congruent and opposite sides are parallel.

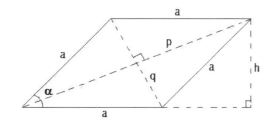

Area and Perimeter of a Rhombus

$$Perimeter = 4a$$

$$Area = a^2 \sin\alpha = a * h = \frac{1}{2}pq$$

$$4a^2 = p^2 + q^2$$

Rectangle

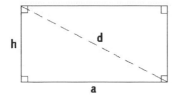

Area and Perimeter of a Rectangle

$$d = \sqrt{a^2 + h^2}$$

$$a = \sqrt{d^2 - h^2}$$

$$h = \sqrt{d^2 - a^2}$$

$$Perimeter = 2a + 2h$$

$$Area = a \cdot h$$

Square

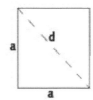

Area and Perimeter of a Square

$$d = a\sqrt{2}$$

$$Perimeter = 4a = 2d\sqrt{2}$$

$$Area = a^2 = \frac{1}{2}d^2$$

Circle

Area and Perimeter of a Circle

$$d = 2r$$

$$Perimeter = 2\pi r = \pi d$$

$$Area = \pi r^2$$

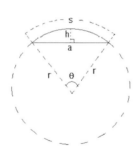

The product length of one chord equals the product length of the other, or:

AB=CD

Area and Perimeter of the Sector of a Circle

$$\alpha = \frac{\theta \pi}{180} \; (rad)$$

$$s = r\alpha$$

$$Perimeter = 2r + s$$

$$Area = \frac{1}{2}\theta \, r^2 \; (radians) \; or \; \frac{n}{360}\pi r^2$$

$$length \; (l) \; of \; an \; arc \quad l = \frac{\pi n r}{180} \; or \; \frac{n}{360} 2\pi r$$

Area and Perimeter of the Segment of a Circle

$$\alpha = \frac{\theta \pi}{180} \; (rad)$$

$$a = 2\sqrt{2hr - h^2}$$

$$a^2 = 2r^2 - 2r^2 cos\theta$$

$$s = r\alpha$$

$$h = r - \frac{1}{2}\sqrt{4r^2 - a^2}$$

$$Perimeter = a + s$$

$$Area = \frac{1}{2}[sr - a(r - h)]$$

Cube

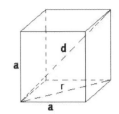

Area and Volume of a Cube

$$r = a\sqrt{2}$$

$$d = a\sqrt{3}$$

$$Area = 6a^2$$

$$Volume = a^3$$

Cuboid

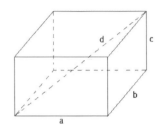

Area and Volume of a Cuboid

$$d = \sqrt{a^2 + b^2 + c^2}$$

$$A = 2(ab + ac + bc)$$

$$V = abc$$

Pyramid

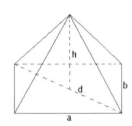

Area and Volume of a Pyramid

$$A_{lateral} = a\sqrt{h^2 + \left(\frac{b}{2}\right)^2} + b\sqrt{h^2 + \left(\frac{a}{2}\right)^2}$$

$$d = \sqrt{a^2 + b^2}$$

$$A_{base} = ab$$

$$A_{total} = A_{lateral} + A_{base}$$

$$V = \frac{1}{3}abh$$

Cylinder

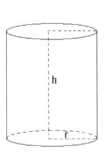

Area and Volume of a Cylinder

$$d = 2r$$

$$A_{surface} = 2\pi rh$$

$$A_{base} = 2\pi r^2$$

$$Area = A_{surface} + A_{base}$$

$$= 2\pi r\,(h + r)$$

$$Volume = \pi r^2 h$$

Cone

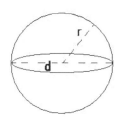

Area and Volume of a Cone

$d = 2r$

$A_{surface} = \pi r s$

$A_{base} = \pi r^2$

$Area = A_{surface} + A_{base}$

$\qquad = 2\pi r\,(h + r)$

$Volume = \dfrac{1}{3}\,\pi r^2 h$

Sphere

Area and Volume of a Sphere

$d = 2r$

$A_{surface} = 4\pi r^2$

$Volume = \dfrac{4}{3}\,\pi r^3$

Test Your Knowledge: Mathematics

ORDER OF OPERATIONS

1. $3 * (2 * 4^3) \div 4 = ?$

2. $(4^3 + 2 - 1) = ?$

3. $(5 * 3) * 1 + 5 = ?$

4. $(7^2 - 2^3 - 6) = ?$

5. $(5^3 + 7) * 2 = ?$

ALGEBRA

6. If Lynn can type a page in p minutes, how many pages can she do in 5 minutes?
   a) $5 / p$.
   b) $p - 5$.
   c) $p + 5$.
   d) $p / 5$.
   e) $1 - p + 5$.

7. If Sally can paint a house in 4 hours, and John can paint the same house in 6 hours, then how long will it take for both of them to paint the house together?
   a) 2 hours and 24 minutes.
   b) 3 hours and 12 minutes.
   c) 3 hours and 44 minutes.
   d) 4 hours and 10 minutes.
   e) 4 hours and 33 minutes.

8. The sales price of a car is $12,590, which is 20% off the original price. What is the original price?
   a) $14,310.40.
   b) $14,990.90.
   c) $15,290.70.
   d) $15,737.50.
   e) $16,935.80.

9. Solve the following equation for a: $2a \div 3 = 8 + 4a$.
   a) -2.4.
   b) 2.4.
   c) 1.3.
   d) -1.3.
   e) 0.

10. If $y = 3$, then what is $y^3(y^3 - y)$?
- a) 300.
- b) 459.
- c) 648.
- d) 999.
- e) 1099.

ALGEBRA 2

11. The average of three numbers is v. If one of the numbers is z and another is y, then what is the remaining number?
- a) $ZY - V$.
- b) $Z/V - 3 - Y$.
- c) $Z/3 - V - Y$.
- d) $3V - Z - Y$.
- e) $V - Z - Y$.

12. Mary is reviewing her algebra quiz. She has determined that one of her solutions is incorrect. Which one is it?
- a) $2x + 5(x - 1) = 9$; $x = 2$.
- b) $p - 3(p - 5) = 10$; $p = 2.5$.
- c) $4y + 3y = 28$; $y = 4$.
- d) $5w + 6w - 3w = 64$; $w = 8$.
- e) $t - 2t - 3t = 32$; $t = 8$.

13. What simple interest rate will Susan need to secure in order to make \$2,500 in interest on a \$10,000 principal over 5 years?
- a) 4%.
- b) 5%.
- c) 6%.
- d) 7%.
- e) 8%.

14. Which of the following is not a rational number?
- a) -4.
- b) 1/5.
- c) 0.8333333...
- d) 0.45.
- e) $\sqrt{2}$.

AVERAGES and ROUNDING

15. Round 907.457 to the nearest tens place.
   a) 908.0.
   b) 910.
   c) 907.5.
   d) 900.
   e) 907.46.

16. What is 1230.932567 rounded to the nearest hundredths place?
   a) 1200.
   b) 1230.9326.
   c) 1230.93.
   d) 1230.
   e) 1230.933.

17. Combine the following numbers and round to the nearest tenths place:

134.679
-45.548
-67.8807

   a) 21.3.
   b) 21.25.
   c) -58.97.
   d) -59.0.
   e) 1.

18. What is the absolute value of – 9?
   a) -9.
   b) 9.
   c) 0.
   d) -1.
   e) 1.

19. What is the median of the following list of numbers: 4, 5, 7, 9, 10, and 12?
   a) 6.
   b) 7.5.
   c) 7.8.
   d) 8.
   e) 9.

20. What is the mathematical average of the number of weeks in a year, seasons in a year, and the number of days in January?

    a) 36.
    b) 33.
    c) 32.
    d) 31.
    e) 29.

BASIC OPERATIONS

21. Add $0.98 + 45.102 + 32.3333 + 31 + 0.00009$.

    a) 368.573.
    b) 210.536299.
    c) 109.41539.
    d) 99.9975.
    e) 80.8769543.

22. Find $0.12 \div 1$.

    a) 12.
    b) 1.2.
    c) .12.
    d) .012.
    e) .0012.

23. $(9 \div 3) * (8 \div 4)$ equals:

    a) 1.
    b) 6.
    c) 72.
    d) 576.
    e) 752.

24. $6 * 0 * 5$ equals:

    a) 30.
    b) 11.
    c) 25.
    d) 0.
    e) 27.

25. $7.95 \div 1.5$ equals:

    a) 2.4.
    b) 5.3.
    c) 6.2.
    d) 7.3.
    e) 7.5.

ESTIMATION SEQUENCE

26. Describe the following sequence in mathematical terms: 144, 72, 36, 18, and 9.
    a) Descending arithmetic sequence.
    b) Ascending arithmetic sequence.
    c) Descending geometric sequence.
    d) Ascending geometric sequence.
    e) Miscellaneous sequence.

27. Which of the following is not a whole number followed by its square?
    a) 1, 1.
    b) 6, 36.
    c) 8, 64.
    d) 10, 100.
    e) 11, 144.

28. There are 12 more apples than oranges in a basket of 36 apples and oranges. How many apples are in the basket?
    a) 12.
    b) 15.
    c) 24.
    d) 28.
    e) 36.

29. Which of the following correctly identifies 4 consecutive odd integers, where the sum of the middle two integers is equal to 24?
    a) 5, 7, 9, 11.
    b) 7, 9, 11, 13.
    c) 9, 11, 13, 15.
    d) 11, 13, 15, 17.
    e) 13, 15, 17, 19.

30. What is the next number in the sequence? 6, 12, 24, 48, ___ .
    a) 72.
    b) 96.
    c) 108.
    d) 112.
    e) 124.

MEASUREMENT PRACTICE

31. If the perimeter of a rectangular house is 44 yards, and the length is 36 feet, what is the width of the house?
- a) 30 feet.
- b) 18 yards.
- c) 28 feet.
- d) 32 feet.
- e) 36 yards.

32. What is the volume of a cylinder with a diameter of 1 foot and a height of 14 inches?
- a) 2104.91 cubic inches.
- b) 1584 cubic inches.
- c) 528 cubic inches.
- d) 904.32 cubic inches.
- e) 264 cubic inches.

33. What is the volume of a cube whose width is 5 inches?
- a) 15 cubic inches.
- b) 25 cubic inches.
- c) 64 cubic inches.
- d) 100 cubic inches.
- e) 125 cubic inches.

34. A can's diameter is 3 inches, and its height is 8 inches. What is the volume of the can?
- a) 50.30 cubic inches.
- b) 56.57 cubic inches.
- c) 75.68 cubic inches.
- d) 113.04 cubic inches.
- e) 226.08 cubic inches.

35. If the area of a square flowerbed is 16 square feet, then how many feet is the perimeter of the flowerbed?
- a) 4.
- b) 12.
- c) 16.
- d) 20.
- e) 24.

PERCENT and RATIO

36. If a discount of 25% off the retail price of a desk saves Mark $45, what was the original price of the desk?
    a) $135.
    b) $160.
    c) $180.
    d) $210.
    e) $215.

37. A customer pays $1,100 in state taxes on a newly-purchased car. What is the value of the car if state taxes are 8.9% of the value?
    a) $9.765.45.
    b) $10,876.90.
    c) $12,359.55.
    d) $14,345.48.
    e) $15,745.45.

38. How many years does Steven need to invest his $3,000 at 7% to earn $210 in simple interest?
    a) 1 year.
    b) 2 years.
    c) 3 years.
    d) 4 years.
    e) 5 years.

39. 35% of what number is 70?
    a) 100.
    b) 110.
    c) 150.
    d) 175.
    e) 200.

40. What number is 5% of 2000?
    a) 50.
    b) 100.
    c) 150.
    d) 200.
    e) 250.

MATHEMATICS PRACTICE

41. How long will Lucy have to wait before for her $2,500 invested at 6% earns $600 in simple interest?
    a) 2 years.
    b) 3 years.
    c) 4 years.
    d) 5 years.
    e) 6 years.

42. If $r = 5z$ and $15z = 3y$, then r equals:
   a) y.
   b) $2y$.
   c) $5y$.
   d) $10y$.
   e) $15y$.

43. What is 35% of a number if 12 is 15% of a number?
   a) 5.
   b) 12.
   c) 28.
   d) 33.
   e) 62.

44. A computer is on sale for $1,600, which is a 20% discount off the regular price. What is the regular price?
   a) $1800.
   b) $1900.
   c) $2000.
   d) $2100.
   e) $2200.

45. A car dealer sells an SUV for $39,000, which represents a 25% profit over the cost. What was the cost of the SUV to the dealer?
   a) $29,250.
   b) $31,200.
   c) $32,500.
   d) $33,800.
   e) $33,999.

46. Employees of a discount appliance store receive an additional 20% off of the lowest price on an item. If an employee purchases a dishwasher during a 15% off sale, how much will he pay if the dishwasher originally cost $450?
   a) $280.90.
   b) $287.
   c) $292.50.
   d) $306.
   e) $333.89.

47. The city council has decided to add a 0.3% tax on motel and hotel rooms. If a traveler spends the night in a motel room that costs $55 before taxes, how much will the city receive in taxes from him?
   a) 10 cents.
   b) 11 cents.
   c) 15 cents.
   d) 17 cents.
   e) 21 cents.

48. Grace has 16 jellybeans in her pocket. She has 8 red ones, 4 green ones, and 4 blue ones. What is the minimum number of jellybeans she must take out of her pocket to ensure that she has one of each color?

   a) 4.
   b) 8.
   c) 12.
   d) 13.
   e) 16.

49. You need to purchase a textbook for nursing school. The book costs $80.00, and the sales tax is 8.25%. You have $100. How much change will you receive back?

   a) $5.20.
   b) $7.35.
   c) $13.40.
   d) $19.95.
   e) $21.25.

50. Your supervisor instructs you to purchase 240 pens and 6 staplers for the nurse's station. Pens are purchased in sets of 6 for $2.35 per pack. Staplers are sold in sets of 2 for $12.95. How much will purchasing these products cost?

   a) $132.85.
   b) $145.75.
   c) $162.90.
   d) $225.25.
   e) $226.75.

51. Two cyclists start biking from a trailhead at different speeds and times. The second cyclist travels at 10 miles per hour and starts 3 hours after the first cyclist, who is traveling at 6 miles per hour. Once the second cyclist starts biking, how much time will pass before he catches up with the first cyclist?

   a) 2 hours.
   b) 4 ½ hours.
   c) 5 ¾ hours.
   d) 6 hours.
   e) 7 ½ hours.

52. Jim can fill a pool with water by the bucket-full in 30 minutes. Sue can do the same job in 45 minutes. Tony can do the same job in 1 ½ hours. How quickly can all three fill the pool together?

   a) 12 minutes.
   b) 15 minutes.
   c) 21 minutes.
   d) 23 minutes.
   e) 28 minutes.

53. A study reported that, in a random sampling of 100 women over the age of 35, 8 of the women had been married 2 or more times. Based on the study results, how many women over the age of 35 in a group of 5,000 would likely have been married 2 or more times?
    a) 55.
    b) 150.
    c) 200.
    d) 400.
    e) 600.

54. John is traveling to a meeting that is 28 miles away. He needs to be there in 30 minutes. How fast does he need to go in order to make it to the meeting on time?
    a) 25 mph.
    b) 37 mph.
    c) 41 mph.
    d) 49 mph.
    e) 56 mph.

55. If Steven can mix 20 drinks in 5 minutes, Sue can mix 20 drinks in 10 minutes, and Jack can mix 20 drinks in 15 minutes, then how much time will it take all 3 of them working together to mix the 20 drinks?
    a) 2 minutes and 44 seconds.
    b) 2 minutes and 58 seconds.
    c) 3 minutes and 10 seconds.
    d) 3 minutes and 26 seconds.
    e) 4 minutes and 15 seconds.

56. Jim's belt broke, and his pants are falling down. He has 5 pieces of string. He needs to choose the piece that will be able to go around his 36-inch waist. The piece must be at least 4 inches longer than his waist so that he can tie a knot in it, but it cannot be more that 6 inches longer so that the ends will not show from under his shirt. Which of the following pieces of string will work the best?
    a) 3 feet.
    b) 3 ¾ feet.
    c) 3 ½ feet.
    d) 3 ¼ feet.
    e) 2 ½ feet.

57. In the final week of January, a car dealership sold 12 cars. A new sales promotion came out the first week of February, and the dealership sold 19 cars that week. What was the percent increase in sales from the last week of January compared to the first week of February?
    a) 58%.
    b) 119%.
    c) 158%.
    d) 175%.
    e) 200%.

58. If two planes leave the same airport at 1:00 PM, how many miles apart will they be at 3:00 PM if one travels directly north at 150 mph and the other travels directly west at 200 mph?

    a) 50 miles.
    b) 100 miles.
    c) 500 miles.
    d) 700 miles.
    e) 1,000 miles.

59. During a 5-day festival, the number of visitors tripled each day. If the festival opened on a Thursday with 345 visitors, what was the attendance on that Sunday?

    a) 345.
    b) 1,035.
    c) 1,725.
    d) 3,105.
    e) 9,315.

60. What will it cost to carpet a room with indoor/outdoor carpet if the room is 10 feet wide and 12 feet long? The carpet costs $12.51 per square yard.

    a) $166.80.
    b) $175.90.
    c) $184.30.
    d) $189.90.
    e) $192.20.

61. Sally has three pieces of material. The first piece is 1 yard, 2 feet, and 6 inches long; the second piece is 2 yard, 1 foot, and 5 inches long; and the third piece is 4 yards, 2 feet, and 8 inches long. How much material does Sally have?

    a) 7 yards, 1 foot, and 8 inches.
    b) 8 yards, 4 feet, and 4 inches.
    c) 8 yards and 11 inches.
    d) 9 yards and 7 inches.
    e) 10 yards.

62. A vitamin's expiration date has passed. It was supposed to contain 500 mg of Calcium, but it has lost 325 mg of Calcium. How many mg of Calcium are left?

    a) 135 mg.
    b) 175 mg.
    c) 185 mg.
    d) 200 mg.
    e) 220 mg.

63. You have orders to give a patient 20 mg of a certain medication. The medication is stored as 4 mg per 5-mL dose. How many milliliters will need to be given?
    a) 15 mL.
    b) 20 mL.
    c) 25 mL.
    d) 30 mL.
    e) 35 mL.

64. You need a 1680 ft^3 aquarium, exactly, for your fish. The pet store has four choices of aquariums. The length, width, and height are listed on the box, but not the volume. Which of the following aquariums would fit your needs?
    a) 12 ft, by 12 ft, by 12 ft.
    b) 13 ft, by 15 ft, by 16 ft.
    c) 14 ft, by 20 ft, by 6 ft.
    d) 15 ft, by 16 ft, by 12 ft.
    e) 15 ft, by 12 ft, by 12 ft.

65. Sabrina's boss states that she will increase Sabrina's salary from $12,000 to $14,000 per year if Sabrina enrolls in business courses at a local community college. What percent increase in salary will result from Sabrina taking the business courses?
    a) 15%.
    b) 16.7%.
    c) 17.2%.
    d) 85%.
    e) 117%.

66. Jim works for $15.50 per hour at a health care facility. He is supposed to get a $0.75 per hour raise after one year of service. What will be his percent increase in hourly pay?
    a) 2.7%.
    b) 3.3%.
    c) 133%.
    d) 4.8%.
    e) 105%.

67. Edmond has to sell his BMW. He bought the car for $49,000, but sold it at 20% less. At what price did Edmond sell the car?
    a) $24,200.
    b) $28,900.
    c) $35,600.
    d) $37,300.
    e) $39,200.

68. At a company fish fry, half of those in attendance are employees. Employees' spouses make up a third of the attendance. What is the percentage of the people in attendance who are neither employees nor employees' spouses?

  a) 10.5%.
  b) 16.7%.
  c) 25%.
  d) 32.3%.
  e) 38%.

69. If Sam can do a job in 4 days that Lisa can do in 6 days and Tom can do in 2 days, how long would the job take if Sam, Lisa, and Tom worked together to complete it?

  a) 0.8 days.
  b) 1.09 days.
  c) 1.23 days.
  d) 1.65 days.
  e) 1.97 days.

70. Sarah needs to make a cake and some cookies. The cake requires 3/8 cup of sugar, and the cookies require 3/5 cup of sugar. Sarah has 15/16 cups of sugar. Does she have enough sugar, or how much more does she need?

  a) She has enough sugar.
  b) She needs 1/8 of a cup of sugar.
  c) She needs 3/80 of a cup of sugar.
  d) She needs 4/19 of a cup of sugar.
  e) She needs 1/9 of a cup of sugar.

Test Your Knowledge: Mathematics – Answers

1. 96.	19. d).	37. c).	55. b).
2. 65.	20. e).	38. a).	56. d).
3. 20.	21. c).	39. e).	57. a).
4. 35.	22. c).	40. b).	58. c).
5. 264.	23. b).	41. c).	59. e).
6. a).	24. d).	42. a).	60. a).
7. a).	25. b).	43. c).	61. d).
8. d).	26. c).	44. c).	62. b).
9. a).	27. e).	45. b).	63. c).
10. c).	28. c).	46. d).	64. c).
11. d).	29. c).	47. d).	65. b).
12. e).	30. b).	48. d).	66. d).
13. b).	31. a).	49. c).	67. e).
14. e).	32. b).	50. a).	68. b).
15. b).	33. e).	51. b).	69. b).
16. c).	34. b).	52. d).	70. a).
17. a).	35. c).	53. d).	
18. b).	36. c).	54. e).	

Chapter 5: Science

The Science section of the TASC consists of groups of information (presented in passages, charts, tables, graphs, etc.), which cover multiple areas of science, such as astronomy, biology, chemistry, physics, earth, and life sciences. You will have 80 minutes to answer a total of 47 questions. Although you are not expected to have taken courses in all the subject areas covered, the TASC does expect you to be able to use your reading comprehension and reasoning skills, as they apply, to the given information. Some questions require you to understand contextual knowledge, expressions, basic facts, and theories about the information. Each passage is followed by several multiple-choice questions. Success is determined by your ability to quickly comprehend the information presented to you.

Basic Skills Necessary

The science test requires you to: critically evaluate data and scientific arguments, recognize relationships, make generalizations, and draw conclusions. Be prepared to make simple mathematical calculations using the data. Some questions require you to understand background knowledge, terms, basic facts, and concepts about the information.

General Tips

1. Refer to the passage for each question. Do not attempt to answer using your background knowledge or your memory of the passage. Answers are based on the data and information presented in the information given, not on what you did in a class.

2. You will have to work quickly. If you break it down, you have approximately five minutes to read each passage and answer the associated questions. Try to take only two or three minutes to study each passage. This will leave about twenty to thirty seconds for each of the questions.

3. Highlight the main points and other items which you feel are pertinent as you read.

4. During practice exams, try quickly skimming over the questions (but not the choices) before reading the passage, as well as the traditional read-and-answer, to see which works best for you. You may find that this approach is not only faster, but increases your percentage of correct answers by allowing you to focus on the key words in the questions.

5. Make sure you're answering the right question and referring to the right data set, hypothesis, or study.

Tips for Individual Formats

The following are tips for each of the different formats, along with the percentage of questions found on the test.

Research Summaries

1. The majority of the questions presented in the research summaries format require you to comprehend the purpose of the experiment.

2. Pay close attention to the experimental or study design, the methods used, and the results.

3. Be watchful for information or hypotheses which are not directly stated in the data that **may or may not** be drawn from the experiment.

4. Be able to recognize conclusions that can be drawn from the design of the study or experiment, as well as from the results.

5. Know how the data was obtained, retained, and displayed.

Data Representation

1. Focus on understanding what information is given.

2. Don't go by memory. Always refer to the visual representation (graph, chart, etc.) for each question.

3. Peruse the presented data carefully, looking for high and low points, as well as fluctuations and trends.

4. Review headings, factors, and/or descriptive facts given, noting the differences and correlations.

5. Pay attention to how the data is presented, such as how the terms are used in each representation (total, control, dependent, independent, etc.).

Test Your Knowledge: Science

Passage 1

Asteroid-Impact Theory

The dinosaurs disappeared at the end of the Mesozoic era, about 65 million years ago. The disappearance took place over a very short period of time and was, according to some scientists, triggered by Earth colliding with a large asteroid.

Today, evidence of this collision can be found in the rock record. Geologists have discovered a thin layer of clay containing a high concentration of the element iridium between two particular rock layers. This boundary marks the end of the Mesozoic and the beginning of the Cenozoic era. This iridium-rich layer has been identified at the Mesozoic-Cenozoic boundary at many different locations around the world. Iridium, while rare on Earth, is a common substance in meteorites and asteroids.

The asteroid not only supplied the iridium, but its white-hot rock fragments also started fires that engulfed entire continents. The soot from these fires, combined with asteroid and crustal particles that were propelled into the atmosphere, blocked out the Sun's energy. The lack of sunlight halted photosynthesis and caused a decrease in global temperatures. Much of the plant and animal life, including the dinosaurs, could not adapt to the temperature change and died.

Gradual-Extinction Theory

Some scientists disagree with the asteroid-impact theory. They point to evidence which suggests that the dinosaurs died out gradually because of a long-term climatic change. Earth experienced increased volcanic activity 65 million years ago. This volcanism could have produced the iridium, but, more importantly, those volcanoes did produce tremendous amounts of carbon dioxide. The increased levels of carbon dioxide in the atmosphere prevented Earth from radiating excess heat back into space, and thus caused a worldwide warming.

The warming of Earth is what caused the dinosaurs' disappearance. After examining dinosaur egg fossils, paleontologists discovered that the eggshells became thinner in at least one species. This was thought to be the result of heat adversely affecting the dinosaurs' metabolism. These thin-shelled eggs, which were easily broken, lowered the survival rate among the offspring and contributed to the eventual extinction of the dinosaurs.

1. Astronomers recently estimated that only 3% of asteroids, with orbits that intersect Earth's, have been identified. This finding adds support to the asteroid impact theory by:
   a) Increasing the likelihood of past Earth-asteroid collisions.
   b) Showing how little astronomers know about asteroids.
   c) Proving that iridium-rich asteroids are common in the solar system.
   d) Showing that many asteroids are too small to be easily identified.

2. A geologist examines a sedimentary rock layer from the Mesozoic-Cenozoic boundary. According to the asteroid-impact theory, the geologist should not expect to find:
   a) A high concentration of iridium.
   b) A high concentration of soot particles.
   c) Evidence of great volcanic activity.
   d) Fossilized plant remains.

3. What do supporters of the asteroid-impact theory assume about the fires started by the white-hot asteroid fragments?
   a) They spread quickly and were wide-ranging.
   b) They removed carbon dioxide from the atmosphere, causing a global cooling.
   c) They burned the vegetation, limiting the food supply.
   d) They produced high levels of carbon dioxide, causing a global warming.

4. Both theories presented in the passage cite which of the following factors as contributing directly to the dinosaurs' extinction?
   a) High levels of soot and volcanic ash.
   b) High concentrations of iridium.
   c) Global temperature change.
   d) Increased amounts of carbon dioxide introduced into the atmosphere.

5. Mass extinctions throughout history often occur in conjunction with drops in the sea level. What would proponents of the gradual-extinction theory have to demonstrate in order to tie those facts together?
   a) Mass extinctions and drops in the sea level are both caused by increased volcanic activity.
   b) The greenhouse effect causes lowering of the sea level as well as gradual mass extinctions.
   c) With less water available, fires run rampant and destroy the food supply.
   d) Drops in the sea level and mass extinctions are caused by the same changes in climate.

6. After examining the 250-million-year fossil record, two paleontologists have uncovered evidence suggesting that the rate of species extinctions peaks every 26 million years. Supporters of the asteroid-impact theory would most likely favor which of the following explanations for this finding?
   a) Some massive object periodically disrupts the solar system, causing comets and asteroids to enter the inner solar system.
   b) The tilt of Earth's axis changes every 26 million years, causing long-term climatic changes which lead to mass-extinction episodes.
   c) Earth's orbit becomes more elliptical every 26 million years; and it travels farther from the Sun, which causes periods of global cooling.
   d) Earth's global weather patterns change in response to the size of the polar ice caps, plunging Earth into a global cooling pattern every26 million years.

Passage 2
In chemistry, the flame test is a way of determining chemical compounds by observing the color of the resulting flame when a chemical reacts to heat. This test works particularly well with substances containing metal ions. An element's atoms, or a compound's molecules, emit a unique spectrum of color when altered to a lower energy state by heat. For example, the element Cu emits blue on the emission spectrum when exposed to heat.

Two students in a chemistry class are doing an experiment using the flame test. The students are given the following chart to complete:

Solution	Flame color
Barium (Ba)	
Calcium (Ca)	
Copper (Cu)	
Lead (Pb)	
Potassium (K)	
Sodium (Na)	
Strontium (Sr)	
Unknown solution #1	
Unknown solution #2	

The students complete the lab procedure. Using a clean test wire, they dip the wire into the first known solution: barium. They then hold the wire in the Bunsen burner flame. The students observe the color that the flame turns and note this on the chart. The students wait until the chemical burns off of the wire and the flame returns to normal, and then repeat the process for each of the known chemical solutions on the chart. They then test the unknown chemical solutions as well. Below are some of the results the students recorded:

Solution	Flame color
Barium (Ba)	Light green
Calcium (Ca)	Dark red
Copper (Cu)	
Lead (Pb)	White/blue
Potassium (K)	Light purple
Sodium (Na)	Bright orange
Strontium (Sr)	Bright orange/red
Unknown solution #1	
Unknown solution #2	

7. Which of the following colors should the students find the Copper solution emits?
    a) Purple.
    b) White.
    c) Bright yellow.
    d) Blue.

8. The teacher knows that Unknown solution #2 is simply a Barium solution. What color should students record in their flame charts for Unknown solution #2 to receive full credit?
    a) Light green.
    b) Blue.
    c) Bright red.
    d) Bright orange.

9. The flame test may not be a useful way to determine a chemical solution for all of the following reasons except that:
    a) Some solutions emit similar colors on the spectrum and are hard to distinguish.
    b) It might be more difficult to determine the identity of a mixed solution.
    c) A contained flame is not always available.
    d) The color emitted by different chemicals can change over time.

10. The lab instructor informs the students that they have filled in the wrong color for Strontium – the solution is supposed to be orange, not an orange/red. Which of the following is likely the source of the students' error?
    a) The students are both unable to distinguish between red and orange.
    b) The students accidentally switched two of the test tubes containing their solutions.
    c) The students failed to let all of the Sodium solution burn off while testing the previous solution, so the test wire had both solutions on it.
    d) The students misread the solution names on the chart.

11. The students find that Unknown solution #1 is white/blue. Which of the following is the likely metal compound in the solution?
    a) Barium.
    b) Calcium.
    c) Copper.
    d) Lead.

12. The students learn that fireworks emit bright colors through the use of different chemical compounds. If a fireworks producer wanted to create a red firework, which of the following metals should be added to the compound?
    a) Lead.
    b) Calcium.
    c) Copper.
    d) Potassium.

13. What color flame would the students expect to record if they dipped a test wire in a solution containing an alloy of Cu and Pb?
   a) Light blue.
   b) Dark blue.
   c) White.
   d) Purple.

14. Scientists have used the unique color spectrum of elements to determine new elements. The discoveries of each of the following elements illustrates this strategy EXCEPT:
   a) The discovery of Radium in 1898 by extracting the chemical compound from a uranium sample and distinguishing the brilliant green flame color of barium from the unknown compound's crimson color spectrum.
   b) The discovery of eka-caesium in 1939 by examining the decay product energy levels in a sample of actinium-227.
   c) The discovery of Gallium in 1871 spectroscopically by examining its unique violet spectrum in a sample of Sphalerite.
   d) The discovery of Helium in 1868 by examining the wavelength of the elements burning in the chromosphere of the Sun.

Passage 3
The coffee plant, *Coffea*, is a flowering plant whose seeds, coffee beans, are used to brew the beverage coffee. Coffee beans are a major export for many developing countries, and thus the best conditions in which to grow the coffee plant have been rigorously studied. The best *Coffea* is generally grown in the "coffee belt" – the region around the globe which is within ten degrees latitude of the equator. There are many different species of the plant with slightly different optimal growing conditions. Below are the results of two studies on the best conditions for growing *Coffea arabica*.

Study I
Coffea arabica is planted in four fields at different elevations. The plants are left to mature for seven years, and then the beans are harvested. Yields of the harvests are recorded. Coffee is brewed using the same technique with beans from each of the four fields, and the resulting coffee is given a rating which ranges from Poor, to Fair, to Good, to Excellent by professional coffee "Master Tasters." Below are the results from this study:

Elevation above sea level	Bean Yield	Coffee Rating
500 m	120 kg	Fair
1000 m	350 kg	Excellent
1700 m	600 kg	Good
2200 m	400 kg	Poor

Study II
Different types of *Coffea arabica* have been found to produce different levels of caffeine in their beans. A corporation looking to produce a high-quality, low-caffeine strain of coffee commissioned a study to determine which factors result in low caffeine-producing beans. The firm conducting the study ran a comparison of different strains of *Coffea arabica* found across the globe. A table detailing this comparison is found below:

Strain	Elevation grown (altitude)	Latitude grown	Percent caffeine
1	500 m	10° N	4%
2	1200 m	4° S	5%
3	1200 m	0° (Equatorial)	5.5%
4	1700 m	8° S	4%
5	1700 m	5° N	6%

15. If the corporation which commissioned Study II makes a decision solely based on the results of this study, which coffee strain will they decide to produce?
    a) 1.
    b) 1 and/or 3.
    c) 5.
    d) 4 and/or 1.

16. If the corporation which commissioned Study II also incorporated data from Study I, which strain of *Coffea arabica* might they decide to grow?
    a) 1.
    b) 2.
    c) 3.
    d) 4.

17. Which of the following is a possible correlation between altitude at which *Coffea arabica* is grown and the resulting quality of the coffee brewed?
    a) *Coffea arabica* grown at higher altitudes produces better coffee.
    b) *Coffea arabica* grown at higher altitudes produces worse coffee.
    c) The best coffee is produced by growing *Coffea arabica* at either very low or very high altitudes.
    d) The best coffee is produced by growing *Coffea arabica* between altitudes of 1000-2000 m.

18. Which of the following is possibly correlated with caffeine content of a coffee bean?
    a) The elevation at which the coffee plant was grown.
    b) The latitude at which the coffee plant was grown.
    c) The quality of the coffee brewed with the bean.
    d) None of these are correlated with caffeine content.

19. A coffee producer is using the results of only Study I to determine the best location to grow coffee, and wants to maximize first yield and then quality. At which elevation should the coffee producer plant *Coffea arabica*?
   a) 500 m.
   b) 1000 m.
   c) 1700 m.
   d) 2200 m.

20. Which of the following may have been an untested variable which impacted the results of Study I?
   a) The technique used to brew coffee with the beans of each of the four fields.
   b) The quality of the soil in each of the four fields.
   c) The elevation at which the plants were grown.
   d) The species of coffee plant grown.

21. If a coffee producer wants to take all available data into account when deciding where best to grow coffee plants, which piece or pieces of data is needed to best link the results of these studies?
   a) The strains of *Coffea arabica* grown in both Study I and Study II.
   b) The bean yields of the strains grown in Study II.
   c) The caffeine percentages of the coffee brewed in Study I.
   d) The elevation, in feet, of the plants grown in both studies.

22. A third study done by the government of Costa Rica, a coffee-exporting nation, has found that higher caffeinated coffee is associated with *Coffea arabica* grown at latitudes closest to 0°. How could Study II be altered to verify or contradict this finding?
   a) The different strains of *Coffea arabica* could be grown at different elevations along the equator.
   b) The same strain of *Coffea arabica* could be grown at different elevations along the equator.
   c) The same strain of *Coffea arabica* could be grown at the same elevations across different latitudes.
   d) The different strains of *Coffea arabica* could be grown at different elevations and different latitudes.

23. Which of the following maps shows the areas, circled in red, where Study II was conducted?

a)

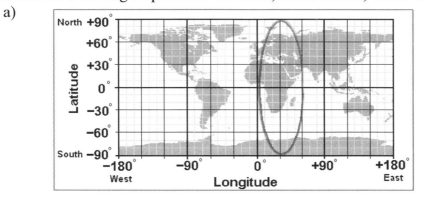

b)

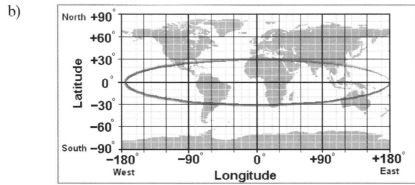

c)

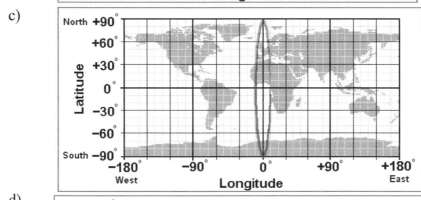

d)

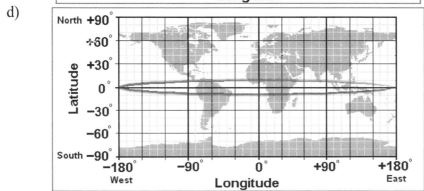

Passage 4

Blood types are used to describe agglutinogens, which are proteins attached to the surface of red blood cells. The genes which determine the agglutinogens a person's body will produce are inherited, and have three possible types: A, B, and O. An organism will produce antibodies, known as agglutinins, to guard against foreign agglutinogens. Below is a genotype showing the possible blood types arising from each possible combination of these genes. The resulting blood genotypes are shown in **bold**.

Blood Genotypes				
		Inherited female blood type gene		
Inherited male blood type gene		A	B	O
	A	**AA**	**AB**	**OA**
	B	**AB**	**BB**	**OB**
	O	**AO**	**BO**	**OO**

Phenotypes explain which genes in a given genotype are actually expressed as physical characteristics in an organism. For humans, the given blood types can produce four possible blood phenotypes: A, B, AB, and O. This is because the O blood gene is a recessive gene, and A and B blood type genes are co-dominant. Below is a chart showing blood phenotypes (in **bold**.)

Blood Phenotypes				
		Inherited female blood type gene		
Inherited male blood type gene		A	B	O
	A	**A**	**AB**	**A**
	B	**AB**	**B**	**B**
	O	**A**	**B**	**O**

24. If a child inherited a B blood type gene from his mother and a B blood type gene from his father, what will be his blood genotype?
    a) AB.
    b) BB.
    c) B.
    d) BO.

25. A person has blood type A. All of the following are possible blood genotypes for this person EXCEPT:
    a) AA.
    b) AO.
    c) AB.
    d) OA.

26. If a population has an equal distribution of each possible blood genotype, which will be the most common blood genotype in that population?
    a) A.
    b) B.
    c) Types A and B will be equally common.
    d) AB.

133

27. If a person has blood phenotype B, which of the following is a possible combination of her inherited blood type genes?
    a) An O from her mother and a B from her father.
    b) A B from her mother and an A from her father.
    c) An A from her mother and an A from her father.
    d) An O from her mother and an A from her father.

28. Which of the following is the only combination of blood type genes that can result in a person having O type blood?
    a) AO.
    b) OB.
    c) AB.
    d) OO.

29. Two students take a blood typing test and find their blood types to be A and B, respectively. The students possibly share which of the following blood type genes?
    a) A.
    b) B.
    c) O.
    d) It is not possible that they share any blood type genes.

30. In addition to the ABO blood type system, biologists have discovered the Rh system for typing blood as well. A common way of referring to this system is with "positive" or "negative;" for example saying that a person has AB- blood. This refers to the presence or absence of the *Rhesus factor*, a type of antigen, on the surface of the blood molecules. Including this factor in the ABO blood system, how many blood phenotypes are now possible?
    a) 9.
    b) 15.
    c) 18.
    d) 81.

31. Blood type is found in organisms other than humans. Apes have similar blood type systems to humans. Felines, however, do not carry the O type blood gene at all. Which of the following tables shows the possible blood genotypes for felines?

a)

Blood Genotypes in felines			
	Inherited female blood type gene		
Inherited male blood type gene		A	B	O
	A	**AA**	**AB**	**OA**
	B	**AB**	**BB**	**OB**
	O	**AO**	**BO**	**OO**

b)

Blood Genotypes in felines		
	Inherited female blood type gene	
Inherited male blood type gene		A	O
	A	**AA**	**OA**
	B	**AB**	**OB**
	O	**AO**	**OO**

c)

Blood Genotypes in felines		
	Inherited female blood type gene	
Inherited male blood type gene		A	B
	A	**AA**	**AB**
	B	**AB**	**BB**
	O	**AO**	**BO**

d)

Blood Genotypes in felines		
Inherited male blood type gene	**Inherited female blood type gene**	
		A	B
	A	**AA**	**AB**
	B	**AB**	**BB**

135

Passage 5

Formation of the Moon – Conflicting Theories

It is generally accepted among scientists who study the geology of the Moon, commonly known as selenologists, that the Moon was formed approximately 4.5 million years ago. Since the Apollo lunar missions of the late 1960s and 1970s, scientists have been gathering more data about the composition of the Moon, leading to several different theories about its formation. Below, two scientists present differing theories of the formation of the Moon.

Scientist 1: The lunar capture theory states that the Moon was formed elsewhere in the solar system and then captured by the gravitational pull of the Earth as it passed by. This makes sense given the composition of the Moon, which is 13% comprised of the iron oxide FeO. The Earth's mantle is 8% iron oxide, so it does not follow that the Moon is composed of the same material as the Earth. The gravitational conditions necessary to capture a body the size of the Moon are precise – it is much more likely that a body would collide with the Earth or pass by it, un-captured. This is not evidence that it could not have happened; that is why there is only one Moon.

Scientist 2: The giant impact theory holds that the Moon was formed when another planetary body, around the size of Mars, collided with the Earth 4.5 million years ago. The impact created a large amount of debris, which coalesced in orbit into the Moon. Estimates tested by computer simulations suggest that the debris could have formed the Moon within a month or within a century at the most. Oxygen isotopes found in rocks on the Moon by the Apollo missions match those found in rocks on Earth, suggesting that part of Earth went into the composition of the Moon. Other compounds found on the Moon in greater quantities than on Earth can be explained by the other body, which would also have contributed debris to the formation of the Moon.

32. Which of the following statements is most consistent with the lunar capture theory?
    a) The Moon does not contain any material from the Earth in its composition.
    b) The Moon is partially composed of material from another planetary body in the solar system which collided with the Earth.
    c) Earth and the Moon have nearly identical levels of oxygen isotopes.
    d) The Moon was probably formed around 4.5 million years ago.

33. Which of the following best describes what each scientist believes the Moon is made of?
    a) Scientist 1: Material from elsewhere in the solar system; Scientist 2: debris from Earth.
    b) Scientist 1: Material from elsewhere in the solar system; Scientist 2: debris from Mars.
    c) Scientist 1: Debris from the Earth and another planetary body; Scientist 2: material from elsewhere in the solar system.
    d) Scientist 1: Material from elsewhere in the solar system; Scientist 2: debris from Earth and another planetary body.

34. Which of the following discoveries would increase the support for Scientist 2's theory?
    a) A planetary body in orbit around another planet in the solar system with the same mineral composition as the moon.
    b) Oxygen isotopes found on the Moon similar to those found on Earth.
    c) Material on Earth similar to the material on the Moon believed to be made from the other planetary body.
    d) The occurrence of Jupiter capturing a small, Moon-like body.

35. The two scientists would likely agree with each of the following statements EXCEPT:
   a) The Moon was formed 4.5 million years ago.
   b) The probability of one planet "capturing" another body is very small.
   c) The Moon is comprised of 13% iron oxide FeO.
   d) The Moon could possibly have formed before the Earth.

36. Scientist 2 makes use of which tool of inquiry that Scientist 1 does not use?
   a) Breakdowns of chemical compounds.
   b) Computer modeling.
   c) Gravitational physics.
   d) Geological analysis of the moon's surface.

37. Assume that the lunar capture theory is correct. How could the evidence used by Scientist 2 best be interpreted to support this theory?
   a) The Moon could have been formed during a time frame over a century, but elsewhere in the universe.
   b) The Moon could have been formed out of some of the same material with which the Earth was formed, explaining their similar compositions.
   c) The gravitational pull of the Earth could have been strong enough to influence the Moon as it passed by.
   d) The Moon could have been captured by the Earth over 4.5 million years ago.

38. The giant impact theory is the one currently believed by most scientists. Which of the following is a weakness in this theory?
   a) Rocks found on the Moon during the Apollo mission carried an isotopic signature identical to that of rocks on Earth.
   b) Venus, another of the inner planets which is most similar to Earth, has a strong gravitational pull and is likely to have also been subjected to similar impacts. However, it does not have a moon.
   c) The Earth's spin and the Moon's orbit are in identical directions, suggesting that the Moon spun off of the Earth after impact.
   d) Similar collisions have been observed in other star systems and have resulted in the formation of debris disks, which orbit around stars and sometimes coalesce into a planetary body.

39. A scientist who studies the geology of the Moon is a:
   a) Selenologist.
   b) Lunologist.
   c) Heliologist.
   d) Astronomer.

Passage 6

There are two primary theories regarding adolescent cognitive development, the psychological development that occurs between puberty and the early twenties. This period of development is characterized by an emerging ability to think abstractly and to reason. These thinking processes are more complex than the concrete thinking evident in children. Adolescents begin to consider points of view other than their own, and to think about the process of thinking ("metacognition"). Two different theories of the process of cognitive development, which can be applied to adolescent cognitive development, are presented:

Constructivist Perspective: This theory, developed by the Swiss psychologist and philosopher Jean Piaget, focuses on an individual's attempt to organize information about the world into structures. As an adolescent learns and assimilates more information, his or her cognitive (that is, thinking) structures advance in a way that allows the understanding of complex and abstract theories and ideas. The theory makes use of a block-stage structure, in which humans must first learn to understand certain types of information before they have the ability to understand more complex information. In this way, humans "construct" their own understanding of the world using tools that they had previously developed.

Constructivist psychologists believe that learning occurs when a human encounters a fact, idea, or experience that contradicts what he or she already knows. The person then attempts to restore equilibrium and fit this new information into the knowledge structures he or she already has. This process is termed "equilibration." Practical knowledge and "real-world" experiences are critical in this process. Teachers function to guide students to new knowledge when they are ready to assimilate it into their existing structures for thinking.

Information-Processing Perspective: This theory, which is newer than the Constructivist perspective, derives from thinking of the mind as working similarly to how a computer processes. The brain processes symbols, which include ideas, facts, and all pieces of knowledge, in hierarchical schematics. Knowledge is organized along different paths: some knowledge is general, like knowing how to walk or gesture. Other knowledge is very specific, such as knowing how to sift flour. Knowledge can also be organized along the lines of how it is used: some knowledge is content knowledge, such as knowing the layout of roads in a city. Some knowledge is procedural, such as knowing how to drive a car. Humans learn by taking in new knowledge and creating a system for organizing it or fitting it into an existing organizational knowledge system. The purpose of teachers is to help students create effective systems for storing and remembering knowledge.

40. Metacognition is:
   a) A theory regarding adolescent cognitive development.
   b) The ability to understand complex information.
   c) The way that a computer processes facts.
   d) The process of thinking about thinking.

41. Both Constructivist and Information-processing perspectives seek to:
   a) Explain the process of equilibration.
   b) Explain adolescent psychology in particular.
   c) Explain human processes for learning in general.
   d) Undermine the other perspective.

42. Information-processing theory is explained in part by a comparison with:
   a) Building blocks.
   b) Computer systems.
   c) Teaching.
   d) Puberty.

43. A psychologist who subscribes to Information-processing theory would disagree with a Constructivist on which of the following points?
   a) Adolescence is the time at which humans begin to think more abstractly.
   b) New information can be integrated into one's existing understandings.
   c) There exist different types of information.
   d) Learning is largely a process of reordering systems of thinking, not of memorization.

44. A child is being observed by several psychologists. The child is given a set of complex and abstract information by a teacher. When asked questions about the information, the child's answers are nonsensical. Which theory does this explicitly support, and why?
   a) Constructivist – the child must acquire more concrete information before she is able to understand complex information.
   b) Constructivist - the complex information contradicts the information that the child already had.
   c) Information-processing – the complex information is procedural information.
   d) Information-processing – the teacher did not help the child to create an effective system for storing the complex information.

45. A teacher who is a proponent of the Information-processing theory of cognitive development may help his students to learn by doing which of the following?
   a) Waiting until all of his students are ready to receive a new piece of information before giving it.
   b) Telling students mnemonics, which are rhymes or acronyms used to help in memorizing information.
   c) Have students work on complex projects.
   d) Ensure that students always encounter information that contradicts what they already know.

46. A third perspective in cognitive development is Behaviorism, which holds that knowledge and behavior are enforced by patterns in the environment and by meaningful repetition of actions. Feedback from others is integral to the learning process, according to Behaviorists. Positive feedback reinforces desirable behaviors, which is how others learn. Constructivists and Behaviorists would agree on which of the following points?
   a) Students who encounter new ideas are learning.
   b) Practical, real-world experiences are necessary for learning.
   c) Different types of knowledge must be learned in different ways.
   d) Memorization and repetition are the most effective ways to process new information.

47. An Information-processing theorist would consider which of the following actions as demonstrating procedural knowledge?

    a) Navigating a city.
    b) Performing an operation.
    c) Reciting the Pledge of Allegiance.
    d) Discussing abstract ideas.

Passage 7

Biological taxonomists are those biologists who order our knowledge of species. Most students are familiar with the system of classifying organisms into kingdoms, phyla, classes, orders, families, genera, and species. Each of these classifications is more specific than the previous; for example, all known organisms are currently organized into six kingdoms. Within all of those kingdoms, all known organisms are organized into around 100 phyla. Species is the most specific classification, with only one known type of organism given each species name. There are hundreds of millions of species of known organisms.

Defining each of the classifications has been a difficulty within the field of biology ever since systems of classification first came into use during Ancient Greek times. The currently used modern system was structured by Carolus Linnaeus in 1734. Linnaeus, a Swedish botanist and zoologists, published *Systema Naturae*, which outlined the structure of a comprehensive system of taxonomy and which, with modifications, has been able to accommodate our growing understanding of living organisms.

On the following page is an illustration showing a limited example of the taxonomy system.

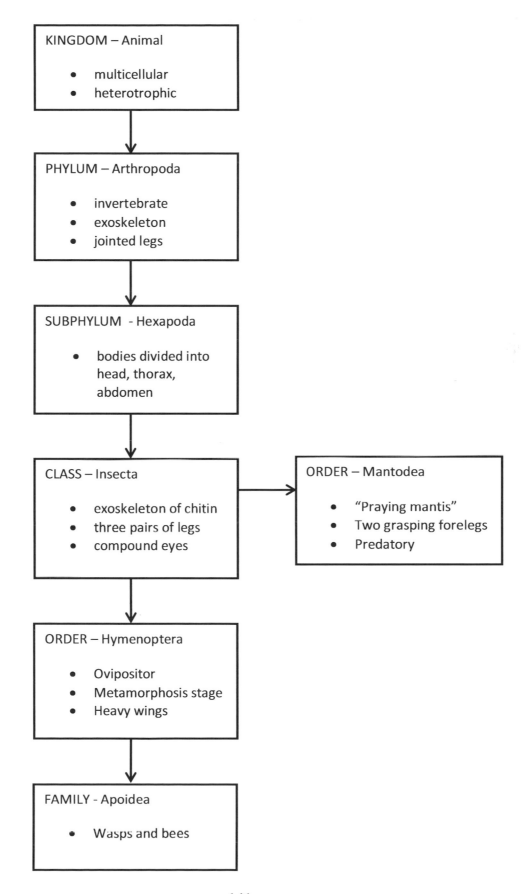

KINGDOM – Animal

- multicellular
- heterotrophic

PHYLUM – Arthropoda

- invertebrate
- exoskeleton
- jointed legs

SUBPHYLUM – Hexapoda

- bodies divided into head, thorax, abdomen

CLASS – Insecta

- exoskeleton of chitin
- three pairs of legs
- compound eyes

ORDER – Mantodea

- "Praying mantis"
- Two grasping forelegs
- Predatory

ORDER – Hymenoptera

- Ovipositor
- Metamorphosis stage
- Heavy wings

FAMILY – Apoidea

- Wasps and bees

48. The most general classification of living organisms is into:
   a) Kingdoms.
   b) Phyla.
   c) Orders.
   d) Genera.

49. Wasps and bees are in the phylum:
   a) Arthropoda.
   b) Hexapoda.
   c) Hymenoptera.
   d) Apoidea.

50. *Systema Naturae* by Carolus Linnaeus accomplished what?
   a) Classifying all known living organisms.
   b) Developing the kingdom classification categories.
   c) Establishing the modern biological taxonomy system.
   d) Exploring the taxonomical classification of insects.

51. Which of the following traits would classify an organism into the order Mantodea?
   a) A metamorphosis phase in its life cycle.
   b) A chitinous exoskeleton.
   c) Grasping forelegs.
   d) Compound eyes.

52. Which of the following organisms are most likely to be classified into the class Insecta?
   a) Housefly.
   b) Tarantula.
   c) Earthworm.
   d) Scorpion.

53. A group of scientists have discovered an organism in a rainforest that they believe has not been previously classified. The organism has a body divided into two sections. Which of the following cannot be true of the organism?
   a) It has an exoskeleton.
   b) It is closely related to the praying mantis.
   c) It is in phylum Arthropoda.
   d) It has a metamorphosis stage in its life cycle.

54. Organisms classified as Orthoptera generally have two pairs of wings and mouth parts formed for chewing. All Orthoptera are also Insecta. Within Orthoptera, there are several different types of families. Orthoptera is which of the following?
   a) A phylum.
   b) A class.
   c) An order.
   d) A family.

55. Given the information in the table, which of the following organisms would be impossible to classify at the order level?

    a) An organism with three pairs of legs, an ovipositor, and predatory eating habits.
    b) An organism with an exoskeleton of chitin, an ovipositor, and three pairs of legs.
    c) An organism with a body divided into three sections, compound eyes, and two grasping forelegs.
    d) An organism which is invertebrate, has an exoskeleton, and has heavy wings.

Test Your Knowledge: Science Reasoning – Answers

1. **a)**

2. **c)**

3. **a)**

4. **c)**

5. **d)**

6. **a)**

7. **d)** – From the first paragraph of the passage.

8. **a)**

9. **d)** – This is not true.

10. **c)**

11. **d)**

12. **b)**

13. **a)**

14. **b)** – All the others give examples of using spectrum testing.

15. **d)**

16. **d)** – Strain 4 has a low caffeine percentage and is grown at a latitude associated with high yields and good quality.

17. **b)**

18. **d)**

19. **c)**

20. **b)** – All other variables are either explicitly tested or explicitly held constant.

21. **a)**

22. **c)** – All other variables must be held constant to test the effect of latitude on the   percent   of caffeine.

23. **d)** – The area between 10°N and 10°S of the equator is circled.

24. **b)** – Genotype shows both genes, not the expressed type.

25. **c)** – Also, genotype of AB would result in blood type AB, not A.

26. **c)**

27. **a)**

28. **d)**

29. c) – The students could have blood genotypes AO and BO.

30. c) – There are 9 original phenotypes, and each can be positive or negative.

31. d)

32. a)

33. d)

34. c) – This would be evidence that the planetary body had indeed struck Earth.

35. d) – Only Scientist 1's theory is compatible with this statement.

36. b)

37. b)

38. b)

39. a)

40. d)

41. c)

42. b)

43. d)

44. a)

45. b)

46. b)

47. b)

48. a)

49. a)

50. c)

51. c)

52. a)

53. b) – This is the only one directly precluded by the organism not being in the class Insecta.

54. c)

55. a) – These characteristics fall into both orders detailed in the illustration.

Final Thoughts

In the end, we know that you will be successful in taking the TASC. Although the road ahead may at times be challenging, if you continue your hard work and dedication (just like you are doing to prepare right now!), you will find that your efforts will pay off.

If you are struggling after reading this book and following our guidelines, we sincerely hope that you will take note of our advice and seek additional help. Start by asking friends about the resources that they are using. If you are still not reaching the score you want, consider getting the help of a TASC or GED tutor.

If you are on a budget and cannot afford a private tutoring service, there are plenty of independent tutors, including college students who are proficient in TASC subjects. You don't have to spend thousands of dollars to afford a good tutor or review course.

We wish you the best of luck and happy studying. Most importantly, we hope you enjoy your coming years – after all, you put a lot of work into getting there in the first place.

Sincerely,
The Trivium Team